# JAINA SYSTEM OF EDUCATION

# LALA SUNDARLAL JAIN RESEARCH SERIES



**VOLUME XII**

# JAINA SYSTEM
# OF
# EDUCATION

DEBENDRA CHANDRA DASGUPTA

*Foreword by*
SYAMA PRASAD MOOKERJEE

*An Introductory Note by*
SATYA RANJAN BANERJEE

MOTILAL BANARSIDASS PUBLISHERS
PRIVATE LIMITED ● DELHI

*First Printed: Delhi, 1979*
*Reprinted: Delhi, 1999*



ISBN: 81-208-1576-9

*Also available at:*

MOTILAL BANARSIDASS

41 U.A. Bungalow Road, Jawahar Nagar, Delhi 110 007
8, Mahalaxmi Chamber, Warden Road, Mumbai 400 026
120 Royapettah High Road, Mylapore, Chennai 600 004
Sanas Plaza, 1302 Baji Rao Road, Pune 411 002
16 St. Mark's Road, Bangalore 560 001
8 Camac Street, Calcutta 700 017
Ashok Rajpath, Patna 800 004
Chowk, Varanasi 221 001

PRINTED IN INDIA

BY JAINENDRA PRAKASH JAIN AT SHRI JAINENDRA PRESS,
A-45 NARAINA, PHASE I, NEW DELHI 110 028
AND PUBLISHED BY NARENDRA PRAKASH JAIN FOR
MOTILAL BANARSIDASS PUBLISHERS PRIVATE LIMITED,
BUNGALOW ROAD, DELHI 110 007

*IN THE HALLOWED NAME OF*

**LORD MAHĀVĪRA**

This book is dedicated to

Mr. Shanti Prasad Jain (of Dalmia Nagar)

as a token of profound respect for his generous patronage of the cause of

**Jaina Religion and Culture.**

—*By the Author.*

# FOREWORD

I have been asked to contribute a Foreword to this book on Jaina System of Education. Anything which contributes to publication of the glories of Indian Culture, no matter whether in its Hindu, Buddhistic or Jaina aspect, is welcome to me. Here is a thought-provoking, suggestive, but by no means exhaustive treatise on the Jaina System of Education by a scholar who has done ample justice to his theme. He has approached it from technical knowledge of the subject. This book is primarily meant for technicians but persons interested in Indian Culture in general and Jainism in particular will find it helpful and delightful reading. The author has given us a good deal of useful information about the Jaina System of Education. The chapters relating to academic degrees and female education are especially interesting.

I may also mention that real service to culture has been done by Sreejut Shanti Prasad Jain by his patronage.

Dated the 22nd November, 1942<br>77, Asutosh Mookerjee Road,<br>Calcutta.

**Syama Prasad Mookerjee**

# A NOTE.

Persons connected with educational and cultural movements of the land might be well aware of the aims and activities of the Bhāratī Mahāvidyālaya, inaugurated only a year and a half ago. Briefly speaking, it is being developed into one residential University on the lines of *Gurukulas* of ancient time and Nālandā–Takṣaśīlā–Vikramaśīlā Universities of later ages, with modern arrangements for education in all branches of human knowledge. It would be built up on an extensive plot of land near this metropolis and a suitable site to start with has been secured on the western bank of the Ganges, situated only three miles from the heart of this city. A few schools and colleges of different types have already been started and a few libraries have also been formed which are being developed for the present in Calcutta and will be transplanted to the permanant site when other adjacent plots of land by the Ganges are secured and buildings are constructed thereon. In fine, it would be to put it in the words of Ācārya Sir P. C. Ray, as embodied in his inaugural address, "a Gurukula *writ large*—a Gurukula modernized, expanded and brought in harmony with the spirit of the time."

Arrangement is also being made in the direction of compilation and publication of different series of books, both critical and popular, viz. (1) Religion Series (2) Philosophy Series (3) Education Series (4) Sacred Literature Series (5) Social Science Series (6) Indian History and Culture Series (7) Language Series (8) Industry Series (9) Agriculture Series (10) Text Books Series, etc.

Two books of the Religion Series have already been published and one book of this Series on 'Hindu Mysticism' delivered as lectures by Dr. M. N. Sircar, M.A., Ph.D. will be shortly out. Some of the books of other series are going through the press and others are under compilation. Volumes of the Jaina Sacred Literature Series are also taken up under the patronage of Mr. Shanti Prasad Jain of Dalmianagar. They will contain the original texts, and translations with notes into Hindi, Bengali, and English. The first volume of this series too will be shortly issued.

It is the desire of the authorities of the Bhāratī Mahāvidyālaya that several professorships should be created for its Theological College in the hallowed names of the prophets of different religions. A few religious bodies have already been approached for the purpose and favourable response too in some case has been received. Mr. Shanti Prasad Jain of Dalmianagar, a great lover of learning and advocate of the cause of Jaina Religion and Culture was approached ; and he has kindly sanctioned a liberal amount for the Mahāvīra Professorship on Jaina Religion and Culture.

The present volume on the "Jaina System of Education," which is possibly the first attempt of the kind, is the outcome of the first series of Mahāvīra Extension lectures.

The second series of the Mahāvīra Extension Lectures will be on the Jaina Philosophy which would be delivered by an eminent specialist in the subject.

A few lines underlying the ideas of the Education Series may be added. It is an uncontroversial truth that the systems of education now in vogue in India, are defective in many respects, which are mainly responsible for the want of religious and moral education, of discipline, of wide outlook on life, besides other drawbacks in the students. The intrinsic value of education is almost lost sight of, and its extrinsic value is now-a-days being belittled due to want of proper employments in the active life. The systems have been criticised on many an occasion, both from the press and the platform, but constructive schemes and arrangement for their realisation into practice are unfortunately lacking. What the true type of education–its methods and applications, conducive to the welfare of students of the land, based on its indegenous culture and traditions should be, requires a synthetic knowledge of the systems that were followed in the Vedic and Post-Vedic, Buddhistic and the Jaina periods by the Gurukulas, Vihāras, monasteries and nunneries and latter on in a comprehensive way by the then Universities of India–Nālandā, Takṣaśilā, Vikramaśilā etc., and of the systems followed by their modern counterparts in India and in other parts of the World.

With this end in view, we place before the public, as the first number of the Education Series, this volume consisting of ten lectures on the "Jaina System of Education", delivered by an eminent educationist, Dr. D. C. Das Gupta, who has gleaned materials principally from the Jaina Sources, supplemented by the Hindu and Buddhistic ones. Many scholars and persons interested in educational activities were present when the lectures were delivered and took part in the deliberations. Distinguished scholars viz., Dr. D. R. Bhandarkar, Dr. S. N. Das Gupta, Dr. B. M. Barua, Dr. M. N. Sircar, Dr. Suniti Kumar Chatterji, MM. Prof. Vidhusekhara Śāstrī, Dr. Satkari Mookerji, and others presided over the lectures.

The book is shorter than it should have been, because of the scarcity and uncertain supply of paper, due to war conditions, and the discrepancy of the paper used is also due to the same factor. A few printing errors have crept in as it had to be hurriedly run through the Press.

Now on the behalf of the Bhāratī Mahāvidyālaya we offer our hearty thanks to the author for his indefatiguable labour and pains-taking researches into an almost new field of work.

Last of all we must place on record our sense of immense obligation to Mr. Shanti Prasad Jain for his kind patronage accorded to this cause. Our hearty thanks are also due to Mr. Chhotelal Jain, the Secretary of the Jaina Committee of the Bhāratī Mahāvidyālaya for his active co-operation.

We may in this connection be permitted also to appeal to other wealthy members of the Jaina as well as other communities for encouraging the cause of propagation, preservation and publication of India's religious and cultural heritage as embodied in the various sacred and other Literatures of this Holy Land, in the manner, Mr. Shanti Prasad Jain, who has set an example in the direction, has been doing.

It is confidently hoped that all readers interested in the subject particularly those belonging to the Jaina community should accord to the book the welcome it deserves.

"Kārtikī-Pūrṇimā"
22nd November, 1942.
170, Maniktala Street.
Calcutta.

*Satis Chandra Seal.*

## PREFACE.

In presenting this book to the public which represents a voyage of discovery not altogether devoid of an element of romance, the author feels under obligation to add a few words as to its genesis and development culminating in a series of ten lectures on "Jaina System of Education" through the generosity of Mr. Shanti Prasad Jain, and under the auspices of the Bhāratī Mahāvidyālaya. In course of his investigations into the field of Ancient Indian Education, the author met with a few suggestive paragraphs in Jaina literature and he went to Mr. S. C. Seal, M.A., B.L., the General Secretary of the Indian Research Institute and the Bhāratī Mahāvidyālaya for a kind introduction to the local libraries containing sacred literature of the Jainas. Accidentally the mutual conversation turned on the possibility of composing a treatise on Jaina education. Somehow, Mr. Seal made the formidable proposal of delivering a course of lectures on the theme. The bare hint turned into a proposal, and the proposal has been translated into action—hasty, laborious, and extremely difficult—on the merits and demerits of which it is for the kind readers to judge.

An attempt has been made on the basis of scanty materials, made all the more scanty by the transference of most of the relevant materials from the libraries to safe-custody elsewhere to survey the theme from several angles of vision—psychological, sociological and geographical.

The title "Jaina System of Education" which the book bears might be more appropriately replaced by "Educational Systems found in Jaina Literature", in as much as the Brahmanical, the secular (Art-school) and the Vocational Education have also been dealt with. It is a historical fact that there was no water-tight compartments in the realm of thought in India separating Jainism, Buddhism and other cognate schemes of life and religion. They all contributed harmoniously towards the development of culture as a whole. Necessarily the contributions of these several systems in the field of education were inseparably mixed up ; and it would have been suicidal to separate them. Hence we have attempted to exhibit the whole picture of the educational life of India in its several sources and supplementing them by cognate avenues of information.

The period traversed in our thesis extends from the time of Ṛṣabha to the 11th century A.D. Many authorities who flourished in subsequent ages but who referred to the period under review have been quoted.

No words can adequately convey the author's immense obligation to Dr. S. P. Mookerjee for his kind contribution of the Foreword.

The author places on record his obligation to the authorities of the Calcutta University Library and the Imperial Library for affording him facilities for collecting materials. Bibliography is attached to the end of work. Finally the author offers his really grateful, and not merely rhetorical thanks to Mr. S. C. Seal, but for whose inspiration, encouragement and patient sympathy in these days of dearth of paper and paucity of readers the book would not have seen the light of day. Inspite of our utmost efforts some errors in prints probably accompained by errors of judgment have crept in. The author will gratefully receive any helpful suggestions from the competent.

22nd November, 1942.
Calcutta.

DEBENDRA CHANDRA DASGUPTA.

# AN INTRODUCTORY NOTE TO JAINA SYSTEM OF EDUCATION

SATYA RANJAN BANERJEE

Any sphere of Indian history will be incomplete, if the contributions of the Jains are not taken into consideration. In religion and philosophy, in art and architecture, in history and culture, in language and literature, and in every sphere of Indian academic world, the Jains have penetrated and moulded the intellectual and moral aspects of human thoughts and ideas for the betterment of human understanding. So also, the Jains have contributed to the field of education. In the whole range of Jain literature, there are some thought-provoking and suggestive remarks on education which can be considered as the Jaina System of Education.

It goes without saying that there were many institutions in ancient India where education was imparted to the people. In the *Manusaṃhitā*, in the *Bhāgavata-purāṇa* and in the *Vedānta-sūtra* of Bādarāyaṇa, there are references to such educational institutions where all types of people used to go for getting proper education. Some institutions originally imparted Vedic teachings only to the Brahmins, but later on in the same place the Kṣatriyas and Vaiśyas were also taken in. We do not know when this system started, but it is said that Lord Buddha joined the famous University at Takṣaśilā (Taxila) in the 5th century B.C. Dr. Dasgupta says that there existed two schools in ancient India, one meant for the spiritual culture and the other for secular and arts. The Brahmins or the twice-born used to go for the spiritual, while others including Śūdras for the secular or arts school. In the *Manu-* and *Viṣṇu-Saṃhitās* and in the *Gṛhya-sūtras* it is also stated that even a Brahmin can go to a secular school after finishing his Vedic studies. There were processes of interchange among the people.

In the Jain canonical literature, there are some references from which we infer the idea of educational notion among the Jains. According to the Jains, the education starts at home in a family. The infants should learn correct speech of their languages at home. It is said that "Goyame received his first training in speech at home under the care of his parents" (*Antagaḍa* and *Anuttara* translated by Barnett, p. 29). In the *Uvāsaga,* it is said that the monks had to be engaged in daily studies. It is stated that besides begging alms and other duties the monks should spend three hours daily for their studies. It was binding upon them. In the *Antagaḍa* and *Anuttara* it is further stated that the princes used to receive their education in seventy-two arts which include, among other things, language, arithmetic, practical sciences and physical educations (p. 5).

The Jains have supported the teaching in art school. At the age of eight, Goyame was sent to an art school. In the *Antagaḍa* and *Anuttara,* it is said, "Then when his father and mother saw that little Goyame was past eight years of age, during an auspicious *tithi, karaṇa* day, star, and hour they brought him to a teacher of the arts. The teacher trained little Goyame and taught him the seventy-two arts" (Barnett, p. 30). "And now young Goyame showed himself learned in the seventy-two arts with the slumbering nine organs awakened (*ibid,* p. 31)". In a similar way, prince Meha was also sent to an art school by his parents on an auspicious *tithi.* And gradually he was also trained up in seventy-two arts.

At a much later time from Merutuṅga (1306 A.D.), we come to know the nature of educational policy of the Jains among the adult kings. Merutuṅga says, "The King Kumārapāla, desiring to acquire learning, had the treatise of *Kāmandakī* on polity read to him for a time after dinner by a certain learned man with the approbation of the minister Kapandi" (*Prabandha-cintāmaṇi,* p. 138). Merutuṅga further says that debates on religious themes were regularly conducted, and sometimes intra-monastic debates took place when learned monks from far-off regions came to participate in the debates (*ibid,* p. 3). In the Debate Hall, the king was the presiding officer. He further says that there were libraries attached to every monastery, and the learned monks used to read and write books for the additions to the library.

It is true to say that the Jains used to set up schools for imparting education to the common people as well. From their literature it can be guessed that there were three types of schools: palace schools, Brāhmaṇic schools and art schools. They all "existed side by side in India outside the pale of Jain monastic schools, each engaged in the spread of culture and learning among the future citizens as preparation for their manifold civic functions" (Dasgupta, p. 4). It is worth mentioning here that the princesses as well as other girls were also educated like princes and other boys. Apart from the fact that the princes or princesses had schools attached to royal palaces, they had a provision to go to the *Gurukulas* for studies. In the *Kathākoṣa* (10-12 centuries A.D.) "We have a reference to a princess residing with her teacher during her studentship" (Tawney's tran., p. 195). "In the country of Vidarbha, there was a city named Kundinapura . In it was a king, by name Bhimaratha. He had a wife named Pushpadanti....they had a daughter born to them....in due course she was sent to a teacher of accomplishments, to learn knowledge, and she gradually became clever in all learnings" (Tawney's tran., p. 195).

From Merutuṅga also we come to know the same tradition. Merutuṅga says: "In the city of Avanti lived Priyaṇgumañjarī, the daughter of king Vikramāditya. She was made over to a Pandit named Vararuci for the purpose of study, and owing to her cleverness, she learnt the *śāstras* from him in a few days" (*Prabandha-cintāmaṇi,* p. 5). Hemacandra has also stated that the princesses also used to receive their formal education from a teacher. He says, "At the king's command, Sagara began to go to a teacher on an auspicious day which was celebrated by a festival (Dasgupta, p. 5). Rājaśekhara Sūri (1349 A.D.) has also emphasized that people used to go to Jain monks for getting encyclopaedic courses of studies—religions, secular arts and physical training (Dasgupta, p. 6).

This brief survey from Jain literature shows that the Jains were very particular in imparting education to all kinds of people—be they *sādhus,* kings, princes, princesses, or even laymen.

The basic idea of Jaina education is to impart lessons to persons in order to build up the character of men and women by practising some kind of discipline in the student life. Throughout its history the Jain sages and thinkers emphasized this point to a great extent. The main idea of building the character of men and women is to build the character of humanity at large, and through humanity a nation is built up. Generally, the Jains have stressed the four aspects of life: *dāna* (gift), *śīla* (character), *tapa* (penance) and *bhāvanā* (good thoughts). To become a proper Jain in mind and body, a Jain must follow these four principles in his life and for a householder these four elements are *sine qua non.* As far as students are concerned *śīla,* i.e., character is the first. By character, the Jains say, one can do all the good things of one's life. There are lots of books which tell us how to build the character of a man. And in order to build the character there are vows which are meant for two types of people—for the *sādhus* and for the laymen. The Jain *sādhus* will perform severe austerity in order to achieve their goals in their mendicant lives. As a result, they will have to follow the *pañca mahāvrata* which are *ahiṃsā, satya, asteya, brahmacarya* and *aparigraha.* Parallel to these *vratas,* there are *aṇu-vratas* also which are to be strictly followed both by the students and laymen. As the Jains emphasize the building of character of human beings, they ultimately adhere to the doctrine of *ahiṃsā* for the practice of which a strong character is necessary.

As studies are the most fundamental and essential to the student's life, the Jains also stress the four *śikṣā-vratas* along with three *guṇa-vratas.* The four *śikṣā-vratas* are *sāmāyīka, deśāvakāśika, poṣadha* and *atithi-saṃvibhāga-vrata* or *dāna.* And the three *guṇa-vratas* are *dig-vrata, bhogopabhoga-vrata* and *anartha-daṇḍa-vrata.* As these are explained in the book, I am not detailing them.

In ancient India, the *motto* of the student's life is the dictum *svādhyāyo' dhyetavyaḥ* which means that studies are to be made with reference to the scriptural texts. To the Jains the *svādhyāyas are their* *āgama*-texts. Out of the 45 *āgamas,* the Jains have selected, at least, four *āgama*-texts initially. Normally, the *Daśavaikālika-sūtra* is to be read first, because it deals with the basic tenets of Jainism of which again character is given the highest position. The *Uttarādhyayana-sūtra* is to be studied next, for in that text the tenets to be followed both by the Jain *sādhus* and laymen and also students are described. After that, the *Bhagavatī* and the *Sthānāṅga* are to be read carefully. To sum up, the analysis of the contents of all these four books, besides philosophical aspects, shows the three different groups of studies: spiritual, secular and arts. The Jaina education says that if a student at the initial stage of his school-life is nurtured under the climate of the above-mentioned studies, the student life, according to the Jains, will be perfect and they will attain deep concentration of mind and will-power to work hard. A student must acquire three *guptis,* i.e., restraint in speech, mind and body. If a student is restrained in speech, he will be able to control his mind, and therefore his body will be free from injuring others. A student must acquire three *ratnas—samyag darśana* (correct vision), *samyag jñāna* (correct knowledge) and *samyak cāritra* (correct character). The Jains say that students must practise *dvādaśa śikṣāvratas,* i.e., twelve educational vows, for their successful career.

In conclusion, it can be said that Jaina education has got a place, even today in the curriculum of the students' syllabus. Unless the character of a student is built up at this young age, it will be difficult for a student to go ahead with his future life. By forming a character the Jains say that a man should be restrained from doing any harm to all kinds of life. That is why, the Jains say that *saṃyamaḥ khalu jīvanam,* i.e., restraint means a (happy) prolonged life. In the modern world, if we follow some of the tenets of the student life as enunciated by the Jains, I believe the student life will be much better than what is found today.

# CONTENTS

## LECTURE No. VII. pp. 61–85.

Education of The Princes :—The Education of the princes from the prenatal stage.—The Child and adolescent psychology—physical, mental and emotional traits of the growing child, and the adolescent youths and their proper care and education.—The Curricula in the Art-school, their psychological basis.—The distribution of art-schools.—The training agencies—72 arts in the Jaina monastery at Moḍerapura—State supervision over the education of the princess—academic, military and physical. Life-long process of physical education—ideal gymnasiums in ancient India—their geographical distributions. State control of the education of adult king.—Programme of studies in the art-schools—method of teaching—individual and group—criticism of blind memory work—five-fold process of study. Educational tour—residence in the art-schools—concluding remarks.

## LECTURE No. VIII. pp. 86–105.

The influence of geographical factors on vocations—their geographical distributions—psychological basis of vocational and educational selection.—The training agencies viz., the Family, the Church, the State, the School and Industry—their closer co-operation in imparting vocational education to scholars—state sanction of guilds and merchants' association—their autonomous status, subject to state control in making bye-laws and in training the scholars in diverse vocations—residence in teachers' house was an essential necessity—vocational education was free and compulsory—and the pupils were placed on appropriate vocations to ensure closer co-ordination between work and instruction.—Concluding remarks.

## LECTURE No. IX. pp. 106–114.

Literature of the Jaina fathers—their medium of instruction—the codifications of the sacred texts of the Jainas—the two important sects of the Jainas—the Digambaras and Śvetāmbaras. A brief survey of the religious activities of Jainas—the parepatetic tours of Ṛṣabha and Mahāvīra—a brief review of Jaina contributions to philosophy, religion, art, literature, history, astronomy, astrology, mathematics, grammar, lexicography, poetics and politics—concluding remarks.

## LECTURE No. X. pp. 115–128.

A brief résumé of the nine lectures with concluding remarks.

## LECTURE I.

## INTRODUCTORY.

It is exceedingly to be regretted that so little justice has been done to the Jaina contribution to mass education in India. It is historically certain that their contribution was as great, significant, and virtually important as that of the Buddhists. The purpose of these Lectuers is to offer an account of the Jaina system of education in India, based on the necessarily meagre materials available. Our task may be best achieved by studying the problem of education in connection with its five important agents, viz. the Family, the Church, the School, the State and the Industry, all of which have remarkably contributed to the spread of education in all its aspects.

The Family :—The family is the nucleus which is ultimately developed into the State through intermediate stages of tribes, the guilds and the castes. The process of transition is the same all over the world, and the ancient India is not exception to the rule. Here too the family, with its purifying, ennobling, and solidifying influences lead to the development of Indian nation and Indian culture. The family, during the Vedic period, when the caste system was in the making, and during the post-Vedic period when the caste system was fully made, served as an important agency of education. It developed a healthy sense of discipline, an ideal attitude of devotion, a peculiar feeling of reverence for the teachers, the father being invariably the teacher during this primitive phase of civilization.

Jainism, which like Buddhism, is not a surd, but an integral part of the encyclopædic system of culture, known as Hinduism accepted the institution of family as an indispensable agent of education and life. We have ample references in the Jaina literatures giving us an idea of the educational activities of the family. We are told how a Brahmin educated at home his sons born of wives belonging to different castes. "Then he had successively four wives, belonging to four castes. Now the son of the Kṣatriya wife was **Vikramāditya**, but the son of the Sūdra wife was Bhartṛhari. The latter was secretly taught in a cellar on account of his being of inferior caste, but the others were made to study openly."[1] The young infants also receive their first training in correct speech at home. Thus little Goyame among other things received his first training in speech at home under the care of his parents.[2] "The family not only functioned as a cultural centre for the formal education of the infants and boys but also it was a school for the formal education of the adult king. "Then on another occasion, the king, named Kumārapāla, desiring to acquire learning, had the treatise of Kāmandakī on Polity read to him for a time after dinner by a certain learned man, with the approbation of the minister, Kapardin."[3]

The Church of Jainas were the first to organise monasteries to preach their religion and culture among the masses and their lead was followed by the Buddhists. Our information regarding the organisation and administration of the Jaina Church is inadequate. Their monasteries were scattered over a wide region in India from the Magadha kingdom in the east to Gujarat in the west, and from the Vijayanagara kingdom in the south to the Kosala kingdom in the north. Gradually Jainism declined in the east and the north, and then it came to be confined to west and south upto the thirteenth century all the time imparting instructions, both religious and secular, to all ranks of pupils from the prince to the humble folk. The Jaina fathers made periodical and systematic preaching tours for the propagation of their gospels. The curricula of the Jaina monasteries were wider in scope offering instruction in religion, literature, arts and physical cultures. These were carefully framed meeting the needs of all grades of students pusuing courses as a preparation for different vocations of life. The Jainas admitted students into their monasteries regardless of caste and creed, thus challenging the educational monopoly of the Brahmins. Specialisation was introduced into the monasteries, and teachers were classified into two distinct groups, some imparting religious instruc-

1. Merutanga Ācarya, Prabandhacintāmaṇi, tr. by C. H. Tawney, p. 198.
2. The Antagaḍa-Dasāo and Aṇuttaravavāiya-Dasāo, tr. by L. D. Barnett, M.A., D. Lit., p. 29.
3. Merutanga Ācarya, op. cit., p. 138.

tions to the novices, and others lecturing on secular subjects to the young scholars.

Among other duties, such as begging tours, the monks had to be engaged in daily studies for at least three hours[4] a day and this duty was binding upon all monks. Debates on religious themes were regularly conducted, and sometimes intra-monastic debates took place when learned monks from far off regions came to participate in the debates.[5] Debates were also held in the presence of the king who was the presiding officer of the debate. Libraries were also attached to the monasteries and the learned monks made valuable additions to the library by writing constantly books on diverse subjects—religion, philosophy, astronomy, logic, and arithmetic. These monasteries were located mostly in gardens in the suburbs of capital cities such as Rājagṛha, Champaka, Śrāvastī, Vanijagrāma, Vṛgukaccha, Dwārakā, Vallapi, Anwilharapura and in other important cities. The sites for these monasteries were carefully selected along public roads and rivers facilitating the preaching tours of the monks and the devotional tours of the devotees of the Jaina Church.

Side by side with the monasteries, the nunneries also sprang up in the capital and other industrial cities for the spread of Jainism and its cultures among the females and these made valuable contributions to renaissance movement. The nuns mostly came from respectable families and spent their time in deep meditation and in preaching the Jaina gospel. Some of the nuns challenged the reputed Buddhist priests during the life time of Lord Buddha, and entered into debates with them on some religious doctrines.

The ruling chiefs, merchants and the public vied with one another for the support of the Jaina monasteries, made liberal grants for the cause of Jainism and the Jaina Church which justified its existence by the assiduity, religious fervour and erudition of the priests. All the Jaina monasteries were under the general supervision of Guṇaśila, the head Church at Rājagṛha, the capital of Magadha. Thus the fraternity of Jaina priests contributed to the dissimination of culture, methodically and effectively in a manner which reminds us of the

4. The Uvāsagadasāo Vol. II. tr. by A. F. Rudolf Hoernle, Ph.D., p. 51.
5. Merutanga Ācarya, Prabandhacintāmaṇi, tr. by C. H. Tawney, p. 97.

monks of mediæval Europe who kept the torch of learning burning in the midst of a surrounding atmosphere of gloomy ignorance and superstition.

The School :—During the Jaina period, education was also imparted through organised institutions known as schools. We have evidence of it in the Institute of Manu where he describes elaborate rules and regulations for the conduct of the twice-born students during their studentship. In the same work the descriptions of the constitution and function of the Pariṣad are also found. From the Jātakas and the Lalitavistāra we get distinct references to organised schools under a University, imparting instruction to scholars, both sacred and secular. The Jātakas refer to the famous University of Taxila which offered instruction in the three Vedas, eighteen Sciences and seventy-two Arts which were mastered by Lord Buddha. From the later source we learn that the Lord Buddha joined the writing school maintained by Vasumitra, offering instruction in 3 R's and Arts or practical Sciences.

From the Jaina literatures also we learn of the existence of organised schools throughout India with a view to imparting instruction, both religious and secular to fit the future citizens for their diverse vocations. The religious schools maintained by the Brahmins were designed for the twice born-castes ; whereas the Art schools were nonsectarian in character meant for the education of all. Organised schools were attached to royal palaces for the education of the princes, and princesses of the royal family. Thus, three distinct types of schools viz, palace schools, Brahmanic schools and Art schools existed side by side in India outside the pale of Jaina monastic schools, each engaged in the spread of culture and learning among the future citizens as preparation for their manifold civic functions.

It is, however, difficult for us to tell with precision whether it was binding upon all students to reside within the campus of the above types of schools. It seems that majority of scholars resided with their teachers. We have reference to a princess in the Jaina literature residing with her teacher during her studentship. "In the country of Vidharbha, there was a city named Kundinapura. In it was a king, by name Bhīmaratha. He had a wife named Pushpadanti ... they had a daughter born to them ...... in due course she was sent to a teacher of accomplishments, to learn knowledge, and she gradually became clever in all learning."[6] Though it is not explicitly stated here whether the princess during her studentship resided with her teacher, we have clear evidence of such custom in Kālidāsa's Mālavikāgnimitram, where it is clearly stated that Mālavikā, the heroine of the play resided in the house of Ganadāsa, her teacher when learning fine arts from him. Perhaps it was the custom in those days in India for the ladies of aristocratic families to reside in the house of their teachers during their studentship and suitable provision must have been made for them for this purpose. The following extract proves our claim. "In the city of Avanti lived Priyangumanjari, the daughter of king Vikramāditya. She was made over to a Pandit named Vararuci for the purpose of study, and owing to her cleverness, she learnt the Śāstras from him in a few days."[7]

The princes also received their formal education in organised schools under a teacher in diverse curricula as a preparation for their princely duties. "On the other hand at the king's command, Sagara began to go to a teacher on an auspicious day which was celebrated by a festival."[8] "The curricula were wide in scope embracing various courses such as the Vedas, the sciences, the arts and the physical training."[9] Hence in the schools the Kṣatriya princes received mental and physical training as a preparation for the princely duties very similar to the Greek youths of ancient time. It was also customary with the princes to receive their education in the arts or secular schools where the curricula included 72 arts—embracing vernacular languages, arithmetic, practical sciences, and physical education. The curricula in this type of schools were vitally related with the realities of life and there is a closer co-ordination between the activities in the school and in society.[10]

The State :—During the Jaina period India was split up into many states. These states, true to Indian traditions, patronised literature

---

6. Kathākoṣa ; tr. by C. H. Tawney, p. 195.

7. Merutanga Ācarya, Prabandhacintāmaṇi, tr. by C. H. Tawney, p. 5.

8. Hemachandra, Triṣaṣṭhiśalakāpuruṣa caritra Vol. II. tr. by Helen M. Johnson, Ph.D., p. 68.

9. ibid, Loc. Cit.

10. Antāgada-Dasāo Aṇuttararavāgiya-Dasāo, tr. by L. D. Barnett, M.A., D.Litt., p. 30.

and other fine arts. The Indian States from time immemorial were great patrons of learned Brahmins, religious reformers, and educationists. The following quotation will support our contention regarding the patronage of learning on the part of the State. "When they arrived, the king caused proper honours to be paid to each of them separately. In the morning after leaving his bed, he said to .... '(What makes you here. Are you troubled by bad men? But there are no such people in this land.) In my kingdom there is no thief, no miser, no drunkard, no irreligious nor illiterate person, no adulterer, much less an adulteress."[11]

During the Jaina period, the rulers of the different states vied with one another in honouring the Tīrthaṅkaras and warmly supported the Creed and did much for its spread and cultures. The Jaina religion made a phenomenal progress in the whole of northern, southern and western India as a result of unmitigated efforts and incessant propaganda tours of the Tīrthaṅkaras and the royal patronage. Princes of the royal families willingly joined the Jaina Order and received their special training for the propagation of the new religion. The Jaina monks lost no opportunity of gaining control over the education of the ruling princes, hitherto a monopoly in the hands of the learned Brahmins. The rulers willingly co-operated with the monasteries in the education of their royal infants. We have already discussed the cosmopolitan nature of monastic education of the Jainas which provided an encyclopædic courses of studies—religions, secular Arts and physical training to meet the growing needs of different ranks of students.[12] During the Jaina period, Jainism was not made a state religion and it was not brought under the Ecclesiastical Department of the State as was the case with the Buddhists during the reign of Aśoka who even supervised the Buddhist monasteries and the religious and educational activities of the monks through the minister of religion specially appointed for the purpose.[13] But the Jaina rulers of south and west India made no such attempt to bring the Jaina monasteries

11. The Vedānta-Sūtras of Bādarāyaṇa, tr. by Rai Bahadur Srisa Chandra Vasu, p. 91.

12. Rayasekhara Suri, Prabandhakoṣa, Vol. I. edited by Jina Vijaya, p. 28.

13. Corpus Inscriptionum Indicarum, edited by Hultzsch, Vol. I. pp. 57, 136.

under the direct control of the Ecclesiastical Department though they made extravagant expenditure for the cause of Jainism.

The Industry :—Finally a word must be said regarding the industrial activities of Jaina India. The Vaiśyas, the mercantile community of India was busy with commercial activities, and were organised into associations much similar to modern Chambers of Commerce of the merchants. Their associations regulated and guided the business activities of the merchants during the Jaina period. Their commercial activities were not confined to the various provinces of India but the rich and enterprising merchants among them carried on overseas trades, thus adding to the wealth of the country. We have ample references of such overseas trades of Indian merchants in Buddhist, Jaina and classical Sanskrit literatures. The inland transportation systems—the riverways, the canalways, the highways and mountain paths facilitated the inland commerce and the distribution of foreign goods imported into India from foreign countries. India was also connected with the foreign countries by oceanways which served as carriers of her overseas trades instead of offering insurmountable barriers. The city supervisor of morals of the youth used to hold a Vocational Guidance conference with the inhabitants of the city and the parents of the youths seeking such vocational guidance used to be present these. We have such reference in the Jaina literatures.

Thus we see the Indian industry was systematised and well organised under a Chamber of Commerce which elected its own presidents and other office-bearers. This association functioned as a school for the training of the youths of the mercantile community which thus sent to the world trained merchants. The Secular as well as Brahmanical and Jaina monastic schools all co-operated in the training of the youths of the mercantile community. We have seen that their courses of studies were remarkably adjusted to their demands. Consequently the young Vaiśya lads mostly succeeded in their profession and made liberal grants to the spread of Jaina monasteries and other institutions of the Society.

Thus from our brief review of the five great Indian institutions of society we come to the conclusion that all these institutions co-operated with each other in the spread of culture and three distinct types of institutions viz, (1) the Brahmanic schools, (2) the Arts schools and (3) the Monastic schools (Jaina) existed side by side and contributed to the stability and progress of the existing social and political conditions of the people. No doubt the Buddhist monasteries or institutions of learning did much for the spread of Buddhist and Brahmanic cultures and their international reputation invited scholars from distant foreign countries. But Buddhist institutions of learning will form no item of our discussion as these are not referred to in Jaina literatures. Perhaps it will be convenient to style our problem "Educational System in Ancient India" as found in Jaina literatures instead of "Jaina Education." Owing to paucity of materials in Jaina literatures it will sometimes be necessary to refer to Sanskrit and Buddhist literatures in order to complete our picture of the Jaina System of Education.

## LECTURE II.

## THE BRĀHMAṆIC AND THE ART SCHOOLS.

Simultaneously with the spread of Jaina religion over the whole of India together with Jaina culture, the Brahmin teachers were equally busy, with the task of dissiminating Vedic culture and education through Vedic schools.[1] A net-work of Vedic schools covers the whole land and through them sacred culture was imparted to students. We do not know exactly when the Vedic education in a technical sense originated ; although the Bhāgavat Purāṇa traces it into the Brahmaṇ.[2] There can be no doubt that the Vedic education originated at home, and it was gradually taken over by organised schools, which, however, did not supplant but simply expanded the ideas and ideals of home education on a sure, systematic and scientific basis. Education was distinctly a concern of the State in the Vedic India. The assembly of scholars or pariṣad referred to in Manu's Institute had a distinctly educational function to discharge. Its members were versed both in educational and religious literatures which constituted their qualifications for performing the difficult task they had to perform.. We also learn from the Uttarādhyayana Sutraṃ that the assembly participated in intellecutal activities. "A song of deep meaning condensed in words has been well recited in the midst of the assembly (nara-saṁgha = pariṣad)."[3] Rājaśekhara, a ninth century scholar and dramatist mentions in his Kāvyamīmāṃsā that the assembly of the learned Brahmins at Ujjain and Pātaliputra conducted examinations wherein scholars like Pāṇini, Piṅgala, Vararuchi, Kālidāsa, Chandragupta and others appeared at the examinations of the above two boards.[4]

The Vedic schools were originally meant for the Brahmins, but later on, students belonging to the Kṣatriya and Vaiśya classes came

1. Sthavira Ārya Bhadrabāhu Swami, Bṛihat Kalpa Sutra, vol. 1, p. 110.

2. Śrimat-Bhāgabatam, Fourth Skandha, edited by Nityaswarupa Brahmachari, p. 142, verse 44.

3. Commentary of Uttarādhyayanasūtram, tr. by Charpentier, p. 328.

4. Rājaśekhara, Kāvyamīmāṁsā edited by C. D. Dālāl, M.A., and R. Anantakrishna Shāstry, p. 55.

also to be taken in. We do not know exactly when this latitude began, but we do know that the Lord Buddha in the sixth century B.C. joined the famous University of Takṣaśilā, (Taxilā) where he mastered an encyclopaedic range of learning including the three Vedas, eighteen sciences and arts. This was to constitute his royal duties both in time of peace and in time of war. The training received here in that ancient university was physical as well as mental and moral. It was meant to make men perfect. The courses of studies were carefully made to take special care of native abilities or "G" factor and the specific abilities or "S" factor : the art courses including painting, music, dancing, leaping, riding the horses, elephants, military sciences etc. undoubtedly took care of the "S" factor. Though these two terms "G" factor and "S" factor were coined by Spearman, a famous British psychologist, the differences between these types of intelligence were known to the Hindus of ancient time and the curricula were especially organized to adjust to the different needs of pupils. Expert knowledge on this head is revealed by Kālidāsa or rather in the contemporaries of Kālidāsa. We see how a distinct provision of a perfect type of education was made for Mālavikā under the tuition of Prof. Gaṇadāsa. Anyway, a sound theory of education pervaded the Brahmanical system of education from the start, the meridian day of education.

The ancient authority Manu laid special emphasis on the mental state of the students as constituting their necessary qualification for admission to Brahmanical schools. We must note here the close relation that existed between the Brāhmanic and the secular or Art school proper. The former was exclusively meant for the spiritual culture : at any rate spiritual culture was their dominant aim. Secular schools were meant principally for the Sudras who might get their practical education enabling them to earn their bread and butter and to serve the twice-born classes all the more efficiently. The incidental reference to this fact is to be had in Manu. "But a Sudra, being unable to find service with the twice-born and threatened with the loss of his sons and wife (through hunger), may maintain himself by handicrafts.

"(Let him follow) those mechanical occupations and those various practical arts by following which the twice-born are (best) served."[5]

---

5. Manu, tr. by G. Bühler, p. 423, verse, pp. 99, 100.

Another authority, Viṣṇu refers to the same fact. "For a Śudra, all branches of art such as painting and the other fine arts ......."[6]

The Vedic and the Art or secular schools were not properly articulated and the courses of studies in these two types of schools were quite distinct. Scholars however could shift from one type of schools to the other. According to Manu it was an essential necessity for the Brahmins to attend the Vedic schools before joining the Art or secular schools. For them Vedic education was a prerequisite for joining the later type of schools. "A twice-born man who, not having studied the Veda, applies himself to other (and worldly study), soon falls even while living, to the condition of a śudra and his descendants after him."[7] Initiation into the *upanayana* ceremony is essential for the twice-born to be admitted into the Vedic school and the age limit varies with the different castes. According to Gṛhya-Sūtras a Brāhmaṇa, a Kṣatriya and a Vaiśya boy should perform his *upanayana* ceremony at the respective age of eight, eleven and twelve. The age limit for each of them may be extended to sixteen in the case of a Brahmin, twenty-two for a Kṣatriya and twenty-four for a Vaiśya-boy from conception.[8] The close connection of this ceremony with the admission into the Vedic school clearly shows that the Brahmin scholars are expected to begin their study with the Vedic courses, whereas the other two members of the twice-born seek admission into the Vedic course after completing the art school ; the initiation ceremony is not enjoined upon the scholars of the twice-born while studying secular courses. "The Veda is to be explained only to one who has been duly initiated", while there is no such restriction with regard to the teaching of ordinary 'language'. The Veda is taught to the three higher castes only while ordinary language is common to all the four castes."[9] According to Kumārila Bhaṭṭa then a Brahmin pupil can easily join the secular or Art school in case his *upanayana* ceremony is deferred upto the age of sixteen from conception and the above quotation clearly indicates this point.

We are told in the Lalitavistara how Lord Buddha in his boyhood

---

6. The Institutes of Viṣṇu, tr. by Julius Jolly, p. 13, verse. 14.
7. Manu, tr. by. G. Bühler, p. 61, verse. 168.
8. Gṛhya-Sūtras, tr. by Hermann Oldenberg, p. 187, verses. 1-7.
9. Kumārila Bhaṭṭa, Taṇtravārtika, vol. 1, tr. by Dr. Gangānāth Jhā, p. 325.

attended an Art or writing school along with five hundred Śākya princes to study 3R's and useful arts from Vasumitra[10] before joining the University of Taxilā where later he went through an encyclopaedic course including the three Vedas, eighteen sciences and arts.

The Jaina literature supports the view that this study in Arts school was justifiable. We are told that the son of Śreṇika Bimbisāra was handed over to a teacher of art at the age of eight from conception. "Then when prince Mehā was in his eighth year, his parents brought him to a teacher of the arts on an auspicious tithi, karaṇa and hour. The teacher of the arts trained prince Mehā and taught him the seventy-two arts."[11] Precisely at the age of eight from conception prince Goyame was sent to a letter of Arts by his parents under whom he studied seventy-two arts, till the dawn of adolescence. It may be noted that unlike the Europeans who calculate age from birth, the ancient Indians used to calculate it from conception. According to modern educational psychologists adolescence for the males commences at the age of fourteen whereas for that of the females two years earlier. According to this calculation it is clear that Goyame completed his course of study in the art school in eight years. It is clear that eight years course was the standard in the art school. "Then when his father and mother saw that little Goyame was past eight years of age, during an auspicious tithi, karaṅa day, star, and hour they brought him to a teacher of the arts. The teacher trained little Goyame and tought him the seventy-two arts."[12] And we quote again "And now young Goyame showed himself learned in the seventy-two arts, with the slumbering nine organs awakened."[13]

The factor of different periods fixed for *upanayana* ceremony of Brahmin boys greatly influenced the admission into Art schools. During the period prior to the ceremony of upanayana the Brahmin boys instead of wasting away their time in idleness used to study in the Art school before they could join the Vedic school after the upanayana

10. Lalitāvistāra, tr. by Dr. Rājendra Lāl Mitra, p. 184.

11. Ardha-Māgadhi Reader, tr. by Bānarsi Dās Jain, M.A., p. 101.

12. The Anta Gadā-Dasāo and Anuttarovavāiya-Dasāo, tr. by L. D, Barnett, M.A., D.Lit, p. 30.

13. *Ibid*, p. 31.

ceremony. This is a hypothesis the truth of which is borne out by human nature itself. There is reason to believe that primary schools or art schools were attended by all the future citizens of India irrespective of caste and creed and the result was that literacy almost universally prevailed. As a typical example we may take the case of the kingdom of Kekaya where Aśvapati while welcoming the scholars who came to discuss the problem of the true nature of the soul referred to this universal literacy of the kingdom "when they arrived, the king caused proper honours to be paid to each of them separately. In the morning after leaving his bed, he said to them "What makes you come here? Are you troubled by bad men? But there are no such people in this land. In my kingdom there is no thief, no miser, no drunkard, no irreligious, nor illiterate person, no adulterer, much less an adulteress."[14] Thus we gather from the Hindu, Buddhist and Jaina sources that the typical art school or primary school was patronised by all the communities of India. Here beside the three R's, the vernacular languages, fine arts as well as psysical and military sciences were taught. The inclusion of Vedic study in the Jaina curricula of education was a ladder step in the right direction creating an atmosphere favourable to the spread of Buddhism and Jainism which stood for universal brotherhood of man and denied the validity of caste restriction.

It is clear that the Vedic school was superimposed upon the Art school, although, the curricula of these institutions were different at the start. The study of these three Vedas and the eighteen sciences was not compulsory for all students. Manu distinctly prescribed three periods when a twice-born boy might drop out from the Vedic school. Thus thirty-six, eighteen and nine years were prescribed by Manu for the study of the three Vedas after the *upanayana* ceremony. According to the plan advocated by Manu a twice-born boy might drop out from the Vedic school after tyelve, six or three years of study in one Veda only. As a rule the Brahmins completed the whole course of study as they alone aspire after leadership in religion. Kṣatriyas and Vaiśyas dropped out after minimum residence. In this connection we may quote the opinion of Kumārila Bhaṭṭa given in his Tantravārtika.

14. The Vedānta-Sūtras of Bādarāyaṇa tr. by Rai Bahadur Śriśa Candrạ Vasu, vol. I. p. 91.

According to him even Manu did not complete the three Vedas and only the cripple, lame or otherwise physically handicapped and the brilliant scholars dedicating their life to the cause of education studied the full Vedic course. "Then again, Manu himself could not necessarily have studied all the branches of all the Vedas and as such he could not always lay his hands upon all Vedic texts."[15] and again "As for the Smṛti text that enjoins the life of the religious student for forty-eight years, this has been mentioned, in the Smṛtis also, only as an alternative course ; or, it may be explained as referring to conditions of life other than that of the prospective householder ; and as such there is no contradiction by this of the said Vedic text. Manu speaks of the person 'having studied the three, two or even one Veda, in due order' ; and from this it is clear that the three alternatives are laid down, either in consideration of the diverse capacities of different students, or as referring to different conditions of life. Gautama has declared that—'with a view to the studying of one Veda, the man should remain a student for twelve years ;' and this is the first alternative, laid down for those desirous of soon entering into the householder's state. And as the second alternative, he lays down the necessity of leading the student's life, extending to twelve years for each Veda,—thus making up a sum total of forty-eight years."[16]

"The longer period has been laid down for those that are either blind, or lame, or otherwise incapable of entering upon the duties of the householder. For such people, there is either life-long studentship, or a life of Renunciation ; and as such, they can very well accept the longer course of study."[17]

The *upakarmaṇ* ceremony (July-August) marks the beginning of the Vedic studies and its termination is celebrated by the *utsarga* ceremony which again marks the study of the Angas.[18]

This period is eminently favourable to serious studies and climatologists are of opinion that mental efficiency reaches its perfection in a cooler climate. Of the six Vedāṅgas, Astronomy may be most successfully studied after January or February or in the spring when the sky

15. Kumārila Bhaṭṭa, Tantravārtika, vol. I, tr. by Dr. Gangānāth Jhā, p. 114.
16. *Ibid*. p. 162.
17. *Ibid*, p. 162.
18. Dr. D. C. Das Gupta, Manu and Educational philosophy.

is clear. The recognition of the influence of the climate is clearly perceptible in the organization of the semesters in the Vedic school. During the time of Manu the Vedic schools were accidentally well-organized. A Pariṣad or an assembly of scholars exercised full powers over the general administration and instruction of the scholars. Rājaśekhara in his Kāvyamīmāṁsā refers to Boards of Examiners one at Ujjain and another at Pātaliputra where learned scholars like Kālidāsa, Vararuchi, Pāṇini, Piṅgala, Chandragupta and others appeared as examinees.[19] These two places according to Buddhist and Jaina authorities were great and flourishing centres of Brahmanical learning.[20]

The Jaina authorities in preparing the curriculum of the studies follow the ideals of Takṣasilā University in embracing sacred with secular education. In their monastic university there were three distinct departments [illegible] Vedic study, Jaina scriptures, and Art. In the Brahmanic or Vedic school Ācārya, Upādhyāya, Hotṛ, Udgātṛ, Adhvaryu, Monitors and Tutors were the teachers of various ranks engaged in teaching their respective subjects. We gather from the Purāṇas and Jaina literatures that the head-teacher of an art school was in charge of the students who used to reside in his house for a specific period.[21]

The Vedic and the art Schools played an important part in moulding the intellectual life of the people of India. The curricula of these institutions were vitally related to the realities of life. The geographical factors govern the course of studies in the schools. As for the financial resources behind these institutions we may note that they enjoyed state-grants and for the Brahmanical schools the begging-tours enhanced the sources of income. On the completion of their studies the students used to pay honorarium to teachers according to their ability. The fee demanded by the teachers in the famous University of Taxilā from the students of royal household and students belonging to aristocracy were 1000 pieces of gold per head.[22] The students

19. Rājasekhara: Kāvymimāṇsā edited by C. D. Dālāl, M.A., and Anantakrishna Shāstry, p. 55.

20. Divyāvadāna.

21. Bṛhat Kalpa Sutra, vol. I, p. 88.

22. The Jātaka or Stories of the Buddha's Former Births vol. II, tr. by W. H. D. Rouse, M.A. p. 194.

of poor families were taught and fed gratis in exchange of manual work, while Manu prescribed to the king the duty of honouring and supporting a learned Brahmin. A Kṣatriya must have in his mind the patronage of learning and nothing more.

The life in Vedic and Art schools was decent, happy and vigorous. The students were looked on as children by the teachers. Residence in a teacher's house was enjoined upon all scholars in the above two institutions of learning. We learn from the Buddhist source that even male students resided in the house of lady-teachers. We quote below to support our claim. "Then a young fellow, a resident pupil of the brahmin lady of the Verahaccāni clan, came to visit the venerable Udāyin, and on coming to him greeted him courteously, and after the exchange of greetings and compliments sat down at one side."[23]

It is not clear from the evidences at our disposal whether female students in Jaina India used to live in the house of their teachers during the period of their education ; but it is clear that they did receive education of a thoroughly effective type. We have even from the scanty materials within our reach a distinctly vivid idea of the vigorous, scientifically perfect and systematic education that was within the reach of all citizens irrespective of caste, creed, and sex. There were no frontiers of knowledge. Sacred and secular learning flourished side by side. The Brahmanic scheme of education supplemented instead of supplanting the Jaina scheme. In a word in ancient India under the fostering care of the Jaina educationists a very useful and practical method of education anticipating some of the essential features of the educational innovations of modern time existed and existed in a vigorous, healthy and marvelously fresh condition.

---

23. The Book of the Kindred Sayings (Sanyutta Nikāya) part IV, tr. by F. L. Woodward, M.A. p. 77.

# LECTURE III

## THE JAINA MONASTERIES :

### THEIR IMPORTANCE AND PHYSICAL ENVIRONMENTS.

The Jaina monasteries played a very important part in moulding the civilisation and the cultural destiny of India, both in its intellectual and moral aspects. These monasteries did for India during a definite period of Indian history exactly what their counterparts of middle ages did for Europe during the dark age of her history. They kept the torch of learning burning in spite of and in the midst of intellectual and spiritual darkness. They promoted the spirit of sweetness, spirituality and light, and developed the sentiments of humanity, charity, piety and brotherhood. The priestly founders of Jaina monasteries were possessed of strong commonsense and foresight which were displayed in the selection of their sites of learning which were mostly in the vicinity of the metropolis, the cities or sea-shores, or on the banks of rivers ,on the slopes of mountains and hills. These ensured their accessibility and popularity, and guaranteed their continuance. People could easily flock to the centres of learning by boats through rivers or could walk through well-constructed roads of which there were plenty in those days connecting the vast cities of India. In our estimate of the part played by the Jaina centres of learning we should not forget the geographical factors : locations, mountains, rivers, lakes, fauna, flora, and the net-work of transportation system which had a remarkable bearing upon the Jaina monasteries.

The curricula of Jaina education were comprehensive and eminently practical, and took into full account the needs of Indian States. It may be noted that every organised State in India needed at least the following departments, viz (1) department of treasury,[1] (2) department of charity[2] (3) department of medicine,[3] (4) department

1. Merutuṅga Ācārya, The Prabandhacintāmaṇi, tr. by C. H. Tawney, M.A., p. 67, p. 170.

2. *Ibid,* p. 38.

3. *Ibid,* p. 81.

of army,[4] (5) department of religion,[5] (6) department of education,[6] (7) department of records,[7] (8) department of foreign relations,[8] each under a superintendent. As the names indicate, the heads of these departments were responsible officers with requisite qualifications due to learning, experience and knowledge of the world. The head of the education department was a superior Paṇḍita with the extensive jurisdiction of all scholars. At his discretion he had the right to expel the scholars from the country for twelve years. The head of the foreign—relation department was a diplomat whose office was to negotiate treaties and agreements between his own State and other foreign States. Each department consisted of gradation of offices very much after the pattern of the modern States. There were provincial governors[9] over the heads of the department; and above all was the king, the sole symbol of sovereignty representing the supremacy and strength of the States.

As in the modern world of this industrial age, a variety of trades and industries, both on large and small scales, existed in Jaina India; and the aim of the Jaina scheme of education was to equip the students with the necessary qualifications for all these branches of trade and industry as well as for the higher occupation relating to religion and morality. In other words, the Jaina scheme of education had the secular as well as religious aspects.

In the present lecture we are especially interested in the departments of religion and education with special bearing on the development of the intellectual and cultural life of the community. We have textual evidences to show that at a very early period of the Jaina history of India the secular education came to be separated from the religious, there being two distinct officers in charge of different departments on religion and education. The superintendent of the Tripuruṣa Religious Foundation[10] in Guzerat and the superior Paṇḍita[11] were respec-

4. Merutuṅga Ācārya, The Prabandhacintāmaṇi, tr. by C. H. Tawney, M.A., p. 148.
5. *Ibid*, p. 25.
6. *Ibid*, p. 52.
7. *Ibid*, p. 100.
8. *Ibid*, p. 41, p. 141.
9. *Ibid*, p. 186.
10. *Ibid*, p. 25.
11. *Ibid*, p. 52.

tively in charge of religious and secular education. This was surely a healthy movement anticipating in fact similar steps taken in the U.S.A. and the European countries in the nineteenth century. Over and above those two departments, provision was made for imparting education to the members of the royal family in the Vedas and other secular Arts. Training in dancing and music as well as training in military arts were taken into full account. Ample provision was also made for training in horse-riding, elephant-riding and other physical exercises. This State patronage was accorded not only to the Jainas but to the Brahmins who maintained Vedic schools exclusively for the purpose of imparting the sacred lore. The mercantile and other artizan communities had their guild schools imparting technical education relating to industries. The members of these communities were allowed to join the Vedic schools and the schools for secular education. By the by the guilds in Jaina India were systematically organized, very much after the pattern of their counterparts in the Middle Age. They made their own by-laws to maintain their discipline,[12] subject to the sanction of the head of the State. The office of the president was in theory an elective one though in practice it was hereditary.[13] As a rule the president was an extremely qualified person versed in sacred as well as secular literature and possessed of a thorough knowledge of the world of men and of the world of commerce and industry. Our meagre information on this point from purely Jaina sources may be well supplemented by Bṛhaspati, who says, "Honest persons, acquainted with the Vedas and the duty, able, *self-controlled,* sprung from noble families, and skilled in every business, shall be appointed as heads (of an association)." [14]

It is clear from the above that the scheme of education patronised by the Jaina State was complete, rational and comprehensive, taking into account all the needs of the community, theoretical and practical, secular and sacred. The educational institutions of all types enjoyed complete autonomy. Of all educational institutions, the Jaina

12. Minor Law Books, part I, tr. by Julius Jolly, p. 154, verse no. 3.

13. Professor Fiélix Lacôte, Essay on the Guṇádhya and the Bṛhat Kathá, tr. by Rev. A. M. Tabard, M.A., pp. 142-43.

14. Bṛhaspati, Minor Law Books, Part I, tr. by Julius Jolly, P. 347, 9.

monasteries again deserve special notice on account of their completeness and excellent organization and cosmopolitan nature of the Ideals.

The Jaina monasteries were widely distributed all over India and in their distribution the influence of geographical factors are clearly perceptible. We give below an illustrative list of the outstanding monasteries in India. In Bengal, Puṇḍravardhana,[15] and the then coastal city of Tāmralipta[16] (now Tamluk, an obscure sub-division of Midnapur district in Bengal) as well as Champaka[17] and Rājagṛha[18] in Magadha were important centres of Jaina culture and learning. Benares,[19] Śrāvastī,[20] Ālabhiyā (Alora), Manivaiya,[22] Kāmpilya,[23] (Kampil in Farokhabad Dist., U. P.) Ujjain,[24] on the bank of the Śiprā, Kṣitipratishṭhapura,[25] on the bank of the Godāvarī, Kollāga,[26] a suburb of Vaiśālī, Paṇiyabhūmi,[27] Kummagāma,[28] Salakotthaya Cheiya in the suburb of Midhiyagāma,[29] and in west India. Nandanavana[30] in the

---

15. Divyāvadāna, edited by E. B. Cowell, M.A., And R. A. Neil, M.A., p. 427.

16. Maurice Bloomfield, The Life And Stories of The Jaina Savior, Pārśvanātha, p. 168. 16b. *Ibid,* p. 70.

17. Mahābhārata, vol. vi, edited by Haridas Siddhantavagis, p. 780, verse, 163.

18. Nirayāvaliyāo, edited by A. S. Gopani, M.A., and V. J. Chokshi, B.A., p. 2, verse. 2.

19. *Ibid,* p. 69, verse, 90. 20. *Ibid,* p. 63, verse, 81.

21. The Uvāsagadasāo, vol. ii, tr. by A. F. Rudolf Höernle, Ph.D., p. 103. 155.

22. Nirayāvaliyāo, edited by A. S. Gopani, M.A., and V. J. Chokshi, B.A., p. 111, verse, 142.

23. Uvāsagadasāo, vol. ii, p. 106, 163.

23a. Cunninghan's Ancient Geography, edited by Surendra Nath Majumder, M.A., p. 104.

24. Haribhadra Sūri, Samarāicca-Kahā, tr. by M. C. Modi, M.A., LL.B., p. 88.

25. Amara Candra Sūri, Padmānanda Mahākāvya, edited by H. R. Kapadia, p. 15, verse, 11.

25a. Haribhadra Sūri, op. cit., p. 39.

26. Uvāsagadasāo, p. 166, verse. 267.

27. *Ibid,* appendix, p. 2.

27a. Jaina Sutras, part I, tr. by Hermann Jacobi, p. 264.

28 Uvāsagadasāo, appendix, p. 2.

29. *Ibid,* p. 10.

30. Nirāyavaliyāo, p. 135.

suburb of Bāravaī (Dwārakā), Polāsapura,[31] Pātālapura,[32] Moḍerapura,[33] Śākuṇikāvihāra,[34] in the city of Bhṛgupura (modern Broach) in the neighbourhood of Narmadā, Vardhamāna,[35] and in the southern India in the 11th century Koṅkonapuli,[36] Kopaṇa[37] Śravaṇa Belgoḷā,[38] Pombucca[39] (modern Humcca), Baḷḷigāme,[40] Anekāntamata,[41] Kuppa-āūt in the Sohrab tālukaṭ, Banavasenāḍ,[42] Heggare[43] (about seven miles from Buḷiyūr in the Chitaldroog district), Śringeri,[44] Kolhāpur,[45] Bandaṇike[46] (also variously known as Bāndhavanagara and Bāndhavapura), Dorasamudra,[47] Arasiyakere,[48] (a famous seat of Jaina culture in the Karṇāṭaka country), were all noted as centres of Jainism in ancient and mediaeval India. The Jaina monasteries sprang up all over India in small towns and villages, devoting themselves to the diffusion of light—religious, academic and practical to train up their alumni for diverse vocations of life.

As we have noted above, the sites of the Jaina monasteries were selected in consideration of many geographical factors, all calculated to increase the accessibility and popularity of the centres of education. We notice below somewhat in detail the geographical factors exercising

31. Uvāsagadasāo, vol. ii, p. 140, para 212.
32. Rājaśekhara Sūri, Prabandhakoṣa, vol. I; p. 26.
33. *Ibid,* Loc. Cit.
34. Merutuṅga Ācārya, Prabandhacintāmaṇi, vol. I, tr. by C. H. Tawney, M.A., p. 136.
35. *Ibid,* p. 134.
36. Bhasker Anand Saletore, M.A., Ph.D., D.Phil., Mediaeval Jainism, p. 191.
37. *Ibid,* p. 192.
38. *Ibid,* p. 193.
39. *Ibid,* p. 200.
40. *Ibid,* p. 202.
41. *Ibid,* p. 204.
42. *Ibid,* p. 205.
43. *Ibid,* p. 205.
44. Saletore, op. cit. p. 206.
45. *Ibid,* p. 206.
46. *Ibid,* p. 207.
47. *Ibid,* p. 209, p. 211.
48. *Ibid,* p. 214.

powerful influence on selected Jaina monasteries and their educational activities.

The influence of geographical factors upon the rise and growth of some of the Jaina monasteries is noted below :—

| (1) Monasteries :— | Geographical factors :— |
| --- | --- |
| (1) Puṇṇabhadda monastery at Champaka. | (1) Water :—inland bodies of water—pools, wells,[49] lakes, ponds, lotus-pools[50]. |
| | (2) Vegetation :— |
| | (a) agricultural crops :— rice, wheat, sugar-cane and lotus[51]. |
| | (b) Tropical Scrub-jungle :— gosiraṣ-sandal, red-sandal, dardara-sandal, various species of trees with right of tap-roots, upper-roots, stems, bark, single stems, thick, broad and round trees shooting leaves in summer, thickets, bushes, bowers, arbours, aśoka-trees, kuśa-grass, vikuśa-grass, lakuśas, chattropas, śirīṣas, saptaparṇas, dadhiparṇas, lodhras, dhavas, arjunas, nipaṣkuṭajas, kadambas, savyas, panasas, pomegranates, śālas, wine-palms, tamālas, priyakas, priyaṅgas, puropakas, rāpa-vṛkṣas, tilakas, and nandi-vṛkṣas were encompasses by many creepers : padmaka-creepers, nāga-creepers, campaka-creepers, mango-creepers, forest-creepers, vāsantika-creepers, atimuktaka-creepers, jasmine-creepers, śyāmā-creepers.[52] |

49. The Antagaḍadasāo And Aṇuttarovavāiya-dasāo, tr. by L. D. Barnett, M.A., D.Litt., p. 1.

50. *Ibid,* p. 5.

51. *Ibid,* p. 1.

52. *Ibid,* pp. 44, p. 6, p. 7.

| | |
|---|---|
| | (3) Fauna :— Elephants, horses[53] buffaloes, oxen, rams[54], cocks, capons[55], parrots, peacocks, thrushes, cuckoos, kobhagas, bhingārajas, koṇḍalas, pheasants, nandimukhas, kavilas, pingalakkhagas, ducks, ruddy geese, kalahaṃsas, water-fowl.[56] |
| | (4) Transportation :- high-roads, junction of three, four or more roads. Vehicles : chariots, palanquins, litters, cars, and carriages.[57] |
| (2) Monastery in the Sahassambavana garden in the suburb of Kampillapura. | (1) Flora.[58] |
| (3) Monastery in the garden of Sankhavana in the suburb of Ālabhiyā. | (1) „[59] |
| (4) Sālakotthaya Cheiya in the suburb of Midhiyagāma. | (1) Flourshing arbour of[60] the Māluka-creeper. |
| (5) Düipalāsa[61] monastery at Kollāga located in the suburb of Vaṇijagrāma which is in its turn a suburb of Vaiśālī. | (1) Soil, density of population & transportation-system. |
| (6) Monastery at Nandanavana garden located in the north-eastern direction of Bāravai city. | (1) Fauna :— Haṃsas, deer, herons, water-fowl, ruddy-geese, thrushes and cuckoos.[62] |

53. The Antagaḍadasāo And Aṇuttarovavāiya-dasāo, tr. by L. D. Barnett, pp. 44. p. 6, p. 7.

54. *Ibid,* p. 1.

55. *Ibid,* p. Loc. Cit.

56. *Ibid,* p. 5.

57. *Ibid,* p. 2.

58. The Uvāsagadasāo, vol. ii, tr. by A. F. Rudolf Höernle, Ph.D., p. 106, para 163.

59. *Ibid,* vol. i, p. 103, para 155.

60. *Ibid,* vol. ii, appendix, p. 10.

61. *Ibid,* vol. i, pp. 4-5.

62. The Antagaḍadasāo And Aṇuttarovavāiya-dasāo, tr. by L. D. Barnett, M.A., D.Litt., p. 13.

| | |
|---|---|
| | (2) Landscapes :—Levels, crags, caverns, cascades, declivities, slopes and peaks.[63] |
| (7) Monastery at Sirivana[64] and according to other authority at Sahassambavana,[65] both located in the suburb of Polāsapura. | (1) Flora. |
| (8) Monastery at Aśokavana located at Kṣiṭipratisṭhapura. | (1) Inland body of water viz.[66] the Godāvarī river. (2) Vegetation :—mango-orchards, containing : mango-trees, nimba-trees, aśoka-trees, trees of varied description, and atimukta-creepers. |

63. The Antagaḍadasāo And Aṇuttarovavāiya-dasāo, tr. by L. D. Barnett, M.A., D.Litt., p. Loc. Cit.

64. *Ibid*, p. 94.

65. The Uvāsagadasāo, p. 118, para, 180.

66. Haribhadra Sūri, Samarāicca-Kahā, edited by M. C. Modi, M.A., LL.B., p. 40.

# LECTURE IV

## THE JAINA MONASTERIES.

### THEIR ORGANIZATION AND ADMINISTRATION AND CULTURAL ACTIVITIES.

The Jaina monasteries were highly organised institutions managed and controlled by a hierarchy of officers. To trace their historical growth and development is a very difficult task owing to paucity of materials. Suffice it to say that there was an Executive Council corresponding to the Senate or the Court of the modern University. It looked after the general administration and conducted negotiations with the State in case of disputes. "The council who managed the temple of Shree Rishub Dev thereupon brought forth their copper-plates and other records to prove, in the royal court, the antiquity of their privileges." [1] We have already referred to the practice of king Vijaya's appointing a superintendent for Tripuruṣa Religious foundation—a fact which evidently implies the existence of State control over education. And there existed a variety of schools under patronage including those for the members of the royal household. Outsiders were also admitted to State schools. The task of administering the monasteries and controlling their policy was entrusted to an assembly of monks with the Siddha as their supreme head. This body corresponded to modern academic Council of Universities.

Śrī Yogīndra Ācārya in his "Paramātma Prakāśa," mentions Ācāryas, Upādhāyas and Sādhus[2] are the three grades of munis. They together with the Ārhats and Siddhas[3] constitute Pañca-Parameṣṭi. According to Kundakunda Ācārya, the Siddhas are the foremost among the Jaina saints and are heads of ascetic bands. "Having repeatedly saluted the Siddhas, the foremost great Jinas and the saints, a person may adopt asceticism, if he desires escape from misery."[4]

---

1. Alexander Kinloch Forbes, Rás Málá, Vol. I, p. 117.

2. Śrī Yogindra Ācārya, The Paramātma-prakāśa, tr. by Rickhale Dass Jain, F.A., p. 2, 7.

3. *Ibid,* p. 53, 299.

4. Śrī Kundakundācārya, Pravacanasāra, edited by A. N. Upadhye, M.A., p. 24.

"He prostrates himself before a (great) saint, the head of an ascetic band."[5] Naturally a Siddha must be the supreme head of a Jaina monastery. Next in order of ranks is the Ārhat. The third in rank in the Jaina hierarchy of monks is the Ācārya, a learned scholar who has reached the highest stage of asceticism. The Upādhyāya holds an inferior position to the Ācārya and teaches the Vedas and secular sciences. The Ācārya is the adept who has reached the highest point of asceticism but has not yet attained to the status of the Ārhat. The Upādhyāya is the master whose chief duty is to instruct others, and the Sādhu is the ascetic who follows the rules of asceticism. The Śramaṇas are ascetics who are versed in the scriptures and lead their life in strict conformity with the monastic rules and are expert in the interpretation of the sacred texts.[6] They also must have teaching responsibility in the monasteries.[7] We have to mention in the connection two spiritual dignitaries—Pravajyā-dāyaka and the Niryāpaka, the former discharging the function of initiating novices in the ascetic fold and the latter rehabilitating the members, guilty of misconduct, in the right course. "That preceptor, at whose hands they accept the (ascetic) emblem, is known as Pravajyā-dāyaka (i.e. the teacher who initiates them into the ascetic fold) ; the remaining ascetics, who help to re-establish them in the right course, when they have committed certain defaults, are called Niryāpaka."[8] Each class of hierarchy of teachers mentioned above had distinct functions to discharge—a fact which will be clear from the following quotations. "It must be noted that all the most obvious and useful duties of saintship are discharged in this stage for example—teaching, and preaching the scriptures, and reading and writing the books, looking after the discipline of pupils, travelling abroad, and taking load.

### THE CURRICULA IN THE JAINA MONASTERIES :—

The curricula in the Jaina monasteries were encyclopaedic, embracing Hindu, Buddhist and Jaina courses of studies. The first

5. *Ibid*, p. 3.
6. Śrī Kundakundācārya, Pravacanasāra, edited by A. N. Upadhye, M.A., p. 30, verse no. 32.
7. *Ibid*, p. 33, verse no. 63.
8. *Ibid*, p. 283, verse no. 10.

group included the Brāhmanic and the Art courses. The second group included the whole range of Buddhist courses and the third group the twelve Aṅgas of the Jainas. The whole scheme of studies was remarkably adjusted to the needs of the scholars of all ranks—the high and the low pursuing secular or religious courses of studies. It admirably takes care of "G" and "S" factors. The Vedic or Brahmanic, the Buddhistic and the Jaina systems especially took care of the aforesaid first factor or general native abilities and the Art courses of the "S" factor or specific abilities. Though these two terms were coined by Spearmann, these two types of intelligence were known to the ancient Jainas which they utilized in curricular construction.

A. We learn from the Anuyogadvāra Sutram that the following courses of studies were followed : the four Vedas, the Vedāṅgas, the Vyākaraṇa, the dramas, the Lokāyata (Cārvāka), Sāṅkhya, Vaiśeṣika, the Ṣaṣṭitantra (a Sāṅkhya treatise) Rāmāyaṇā, Bhīmasuruksha, Kauṭilya's Arthaśāstra, Treatment of horses, the Science of chariots, Kārpāsika Śāstras, Nāgasūkshmā, Kanaka-saptati śāstrā, etc.

B. Buddha Śāsana (the Doctrins of Buddha).

C. The seventy-two Arts.[9] (These will be discussed in connection with the education of the princes.)

D. The twelve Aṅgas of the Jainas which are as follows :—

1. Ācārāṅga Sūtra.
2. Sūtrakṛtāṅga.
3. Sthānaṅga.
4. Samavāyāṅga.
5. Vyākhyā Prajñapti.
6. Jñātādharma-kathāḥ.
7. Upāsakadaśāḥ.
8. Antakṛddaśāḥ.
9. Anuttaraupapātikadaśāḥ.
10. Praśna-Vyākaraṇāṁ.
11. Vipāka-Śūtram.
12. Dṛṣṭivāda.[10]

We do not know for certain which of the Jaina monasteries offered

9. Anuyogadvāra-Sūtra, p. 30. 10. Anuyogadvāra-Sūtra, p. 32.

the encyclopaedic curricula including the Brahmanic, the Arts as well as the Jaina courses of studies. We learn however from the Prabandha Koṣa, vol. 1 that the seventy-two Arts, including the Vedas, the Vedāṅgas, Fine-Arts, Military sciences, and other scientific courses were offered to Āma, prince of Kanauj, son of king Yaśovarman at the Jaina monastery at the city of Morera in Guzerat by Siddhasena.[11] It is however quite likely that all the important Jaina monasteries offered the whole range of encyclopaedic courses of studies with modifications to suit the needs of local society and individuals. We have not materials at our disposal to prove our contention. But we learn from stray references in the Jaina scriptures that eleven of the twelve Aṅgas were offered in the following Jaina monasteries :—

(1) Campā :—In the Posaha-house at Campaka, Kāmadeva, received instruction in the Law from Mahāvīra, his spiritual master.[12]

(2) Rājagṛha :—The eleven Aṅgas were also taught to novices, young or adult, in the Gunaśila sanctuary at Rājagṛha. There a rich man of the name of Makai renounced the world and took to monastic life and studied the scriptures.[13]

(3) Vaiśālī :—At Kollāga, a suburb of Vāṇijagrāma which was in its turn a suburb of Vaiśālī, a householder of the name of Ānanda directly became a disciple of Lord Mahāvīra with some characteristic expressions of piety and devotion.[14]

(4) Benares :—The Jaina sanctuary, Kāma-Mahāvana at Bārāṇasī offered instructions in the eleven Aṅgas. It is stated that King Ālakkha of the above city joined, on his retirement from active life, the monastic order and devoted himself to an arduous course of studies.[15]

(5) In the city of Śrāvastī which was a centre of spiritual culture,

---

11. Rājaśekhara, Prabandhakośa, vol. I, p. 27.

12. Uvāsagadasāo, vol. I, tr. by A. F. Rudolf Höernle, p. 81.

13. The Antagaḍadasāo And Anuttarovavāiyā Dasāo, tr. by L. D. Barnett, M.A., D.Lit., p. 85.

14. The Uvāsagadasāo, vol. I, tr. by A. F. Rudolf Höernle, pp. 6-10.

15. The Antagaḍadasāo And Anuttarovavāiyā Dasāo, tr. by L. D. Barnett, M.A., D.Lit., p. 96.

a devoted student named Aṅgai, formerly a rich merchant, thoroughly mastered the scriptures under Pārśva.[16]

(6) In an unidentified Indian town of Maṇicaiya was a Jaina temple named Taraina. Puṇṇabhadda, a rich citizen of this city studied the eleven Aṅgas[17] under the elderly monks.[17]

(7) Bāravai (Dvārakā) :—Prince Niṣadha, son of Baḷadeva,, king of Bāravai and his wife Revaī embraced asceticism under Lord Ariṭṭanemi at Nandanavana and studied the eleven Aṅgas of the Jainas under the competent disciples of Lord Ariṭṭanemi. "Then that houseless monk Niṣadha studied the eleven Aṅgas under such worthy elderly disciples of Lord Ariṭṭanemi as Samaiya and others."[18]

(8) Polāsapura :—In the Śirivana park within the vicinity of Polāsapura prince Ainutta studied the laws of peace and the eleven Aṅgas under Lord Goyama. "He studied the Law of peace and rest, and the eleven Aṅgas."[19]

(9) Kṣitipratiṣṭhāpura :—There lived Vijayasena, a Jaina teacher versed in the twelve canonical laws in the Aśokavana monastery in the city of Kṣitipratiṣṭhā on the bank of the river Godāvarī.[20]

Thus our brief review of the teaching of the Aṅgas in the Jaina monasteries clearly proves that at least eleven of the twelve Aṅgas of the Jainas were taught to students destined for church services. We do not exactly know which monasteries except the one at Morerapura offered instructions in the encyclopaedic curricula given here. It is however certain that all the leading monasteries, especially the ones located in capital cities, in commercial centres and other important places made provision for teaching the whole of the vast course embraced in the ideal type of education.

---

16. The Antagaḍadasāo And Anuttarovavāiyā Dasāo, tr. by L. D. Barnett, M.A., D.Lit., p. 63. verse no. 81.

17. The Nirāyavalī, edited by A. S. Gopāni, M.A., and V. J. Chokshi, B.A., pp. 110-111, verse nos. 142-43.

18. *Ibid,* p. 136, verse no. 186.

19. The Antagaḍadasāo And Anuttarovavāiyā Dasāo, tr. by L. D. Barnett, M.A., D.Lit., pp. 94-96.

20. Haribhadra Sūri, Samarāicca-kahā, edited by M. C. Modi, M.A., LL.B., p. 39.

*Education in the Jaina Monasteries* :—

We have no definite knowledge of the exact rules governing semesters or sessions in the Jaina monasteries, but from the inclusion of the Vedic courses of studies in the Jaina curricula, we feel pretty sure that the Vedic rules on this head were wholly introduced by the Jaina educationists with certain modifications due to the peculiar nature of the case. True to the Jaina ideal, all rules and regulations relating to castes were totally abolished. Students of all communities and all religions were admitted into Jaina monasteries. In their educational method the Jaina authorities totally disapproved the blind memory method and emphasized the appeal to reason. They realised full well that the aim of education should be to develop the latent faculties of mind and not to tax the memory of the student. "You are only bearer of words as it were, you do not understand their meaning, though you have learned the Vedas."[21] Similar views were expressed by Lord Buddha and Michael de Montaigne, the seventeenth century French scholar. "Many deluded men learned the doctrine in all its different branches and having so learnt this doctrine, they do not go to enquire wisely into its meaning; and not reaching to its meaning, they fail to attain insight. Lacking in wisdom, they learn the doctrine only with a view to quoting texts for the sake of advantage in argument........ In the self-same way, many a foolish deluded man learns the doctrines only that he may argue and dispute about them, never enquiring into their real meaning."[22] The famous French scholar, Michael de Montaigne condemns cramming in the following words: "We only toil and labour to stuff the memory, and in the meantime leave the conscience and the understanding unfurnished and void. And like birds who fly abroad to forage for grain and bring it home in their beak without tasting it themselves, to feed their young, so our pedants go picking knowledge here and there out of several authors, and hold it at their tongue's end, only to distribute it amongst their pupils."[23] We are agreeably surprised to find three very distinguished personalities independently holding almost identically the same views

21. Jaina Sūtras, vol. II. tr. by Hermann Jacobi, p. 52.
22. Majjhimanikāya, tr. by Bhikkhū Silacara, pp. 167-168.
23. Michael De Montaigue, Essays, tr. by C. Cotton, pp. 54-55.

in a very vitally important point in education. These views are diametrically opposed to the views that prevail in the field of education in the modern world of to-day in practice and not in theory.

The method of study that prevailed in the Jaina monastery was a comprehensive and rational one, there being five steps in the passage of the acquisition of knowledge, namely, rehearsal, repetition, interrogation, concentration and discussion. Study is fivefold : saying or learning one's lesson ; questioning the teacher about it, repetition, pondering, and religious discourse.[24] The Jaina teachers especially valued the influence of repetition in imparting knowledge and the very word repeatedly occurs in the sacred text.[25] Over and above, following the method of five steps, the Jaina authorities utilized the biographical method in their extension lectures. They used to utilise a real or fictitious personality as a peg round which to weave their lessons on literary and moral subjects.

There is reason to believe that the Jaina monasteries made special provisions for the military and physical education of the princes and the children of the military classes. Invariably there was either a field attached to every monastery for the exercise of military students or there were public gardens reserved exclusively for this purpose ; these were utilized by the monks to offer military instructions to their pupils. As in a modern military school, here the princes learnt military warfare from their professors, who in spite of their being monks, were versed in military arts. The teachers used to suggest remedies for pointing out defect in their movements and so forth. In teaching military science the teachers adapted their course of training to the mental aptitude of the students. We can get a clear glimpse into the state of things that prevailed in the field of military education in Jaina India. "He exhibited to the Lord the shooting of a doll on a wheel, shooting an invisible object by sound, the shooting at a target in water, the shooting of a clay-ball on a wheel with arrows, who showed *pādagati,* carrying a sword and shield, having entered the shield like the moon in a cloud. He whirled rapidly a lance, spear, and club, giving the appearance of a fiery streak of lighting, revolving in the sky. He showed him knife-science with

24. Jaina Sūtras, vol. II. tr. by Hermann Jacobi, p. 179, 4.

25. Śrī Yogindra Ācārya, Paramātma-prakāśa, tr. by Rickhab Dass Jain, B.A., p. 59, 341.

all the knife-positions, expert in all the steps, like a dancer showing a dance. From devotion to his teacher and a desire to be taught by him showed Ajita Svāmin his skill in other weapons also. Whatever was lacking in Sagara's arts the Master taught him. For such a man had such a teacher. So both, engaged in activities according to their natures, crossed the first period of life, and travelled crossing the boundary of a village."[26]

The admission to the Jaina monasteries, exactly followed the method of admission to the Vedic schools, there being an officer with the title of Pravajyā-dāyaka who initiated the novices into the aecetic fold and there being another officer who looked after their moral conduct. The title of the latter was Niryāpaka. We learn from the Pravacanasāra and the Mulācāra Sūtra that an ethical code of conduct of a very strict type was applied to the guidance of novices of Jaina monasteries. Special respect was to be shown to teachers, senior monks and guests. "Standing up (when the elderly monks arrive), following them (when they are going), showing respect (to them) and removal of fatigue: these, accompanied by salutation and adoration, are not forbidden for monks having auspicious resultant of consciousness."[27]

The Śramaṇas with concentrated mind, moral discipline and faith must regularly study the scriptures. "He, who is simultaneously applied to (the cultivation of) the trio of right faith, knowledge and conduct, is said to have attained concentration; and he has perfect asceticism."[28] The Jaina fathers consider the study of the scriptures to be of supreme importance. "Application to the (study of) scriptures is of the highest importance."[29] The students of Jaina monasteries received their education, boarding and lodging free. Begging-tours were prescribed for the students. The teachers were required to follow a prescribed scheme of duties, which will be evident from the following quotations: "Preaching alone right faith and knowledge, receiving and feeding the pupils and giving instruction in the worship

---

26. Hemacandra: Trisaṣtiśalākāpuruṣacarita, vol. II, tr. by Helen M. Johnson, Ph.D. p. 71.

27. Śri Kundakundācārya: Pravacanasāra, edited by A. N. Upadhye, M.A. p. 32., verse 47.

28. *Ibid,* p. 30, verse 42.

29. *Ibid,* p. 30, verse 32.

of great Jins constitute the course of conduct of monks with auspicious resultant of consciousness. In addition to the above duty, the following ten commandments are prescribed for the ascetics by the great Jinas. Violation of any of these commandments amounts to a default on their part. "Five vows, fivefold carefulness, control of five senses, pulling out of the hair, sixfold Āvaśyaka or essential nakedness, not taking bath, sleeping on ground, not cleaning the teeth, taking meals in standing posture and taking only one meal a day—these, in fact, have been prescribed, as the primary virtues of the ascetic, by the great Jinas."[30]

Mention is constantly made of various grades of academic honours such as the diploma of Paṇḍita, Bahuśruta and Doctorate degrees. Like the modern Universities, the Jaina fathers used to confer degrees on successful students. The title of Paṇḍita used to be conferred on successful students of moderate attainments. It was by no means the highest degree in the Jaina University. Such a title used to be conferred on scholars of the Vikramaśīla University by the kings of Bengal. "Darauf wurde ihm zur Zeit des Königs Mahāpala ein schöner Aufenthaltsort, namens Vikramaçila bewahrt."[31] We learn of this title from the Mahābhārata and the Buddhist sources ; and the definitions contained therein do not show it to be the highest academic honour. It used to be conferred upon scholars not so much for their erudition and depth of learning as for their asceticism and purity of character. The Jaina temple of Ariṣṭanemi in Kaṇavatī, Guzerat, had paṇḍits attached to it.[32] The inferiority of the diploma of paṇḍita to a doctorate will be clear from the following quotation : "Representatives of all sects were summoned to revise the panegyric, and the teacher Hemacandra sent there his subordinate disciple the paṇḍita Rāmacandra."[33] In the Vedic schools, too, the diploma of *Paṇḍita* did not indicate the highest type of honour. This title used to be conferred upon a student studying in a Vedic school. This view is corroborated by the following quotation. "She was made

30. Śrī Kundakundācārya, Pravacanasāra, edited by A. N. Upadhye, M.A. p. 25, verses. 8-9.

31. Tāranātha, Geschichte des Buddhismus in Indien, tr. by Schiefner, p. 232.

32. Merutuṅga Ācārya, Prabandhacintāmaṇi, tr. by C. H. Tawney, M.A., p. 97.

33. *Ibid.*, p. 93.

over to a Paṇḍita named Vararuci for the purpose of study,"[34] Originally meant to signify asceticism, the title *Paṇḍita* came gradually to denote scholarship. The process of transition will be clear from the words of Lord Buddha: "He, who after examining both kinds of senses, internally and externally, is endowed with a clear understanding and has conquerred evil and good (kaṇhasukka), such a one is called a Paṇḍita (wise) by being so."[35] Buddhaghoṣa seems to support this view of Lord Buddha. His expression "paṇḍiccaṃ" is equivalent to erudition. We quote below from Buddhaghoṣa', "Where the *substantival* form, *paṇḍiccaṃ,* is renderd 'erudition', and paraphrased (Asl. 147) as *paṇḍitassa bhāvo,* the state of a wise person, one who was discernment, discretion, one who has 'chosen that good part' as contrasted with the 'average sensual person' or foolish youth."[36] According to Jaina authorities, as we have noted, it referred to asceticism. Gradually at a much later period, the diploma of Paṇḍita came to signify academic honour, and it used to be conferred even upon females on account of their scholarship and proficiency in all the sciences.[37]

*The Master's degree* :— The Jaina literature proper does not give us any explicit reference to the Master's degree, although we have a good deal of information about it from the Buddhistic sources. The following quotation proves the existence of Master's degree in Buddhist India during the life-time of Lord Buddha. "He is a master of logical analysis; a master in analyzing causal relations; a master of grammatical analysis; master in analyzing things knowable."[38] It is probable, though it is not certain, that the Jainas followed the Buddhist practice of conferring Master's degree on competent candidates. We have it on record that the Buddhist Universities conferred the honour on the deserving candidates during the life-time of the Buddha himself. In the seventh century, the famous University of Nālandā used to confer this honour upon competent students. Above the Master's degree

---

34. Merutuṅga Ācārya, Prabandhacintāmaṇi, tr. by C. H. Tawney, M.A., p. 5.

35. The Sutta-Nipāta, tr. by V. Fausböll, p. 90.

36a. Buddhaghosa, The Expositor, vol. I, tr. by Maung Tin, M.A., p. 330.

36b. The Attanagalu-Vaṁsa, tr. by James D'Alwis, M.R.A.S., pp. 23-24.

37. Hemacandrācārya, The Yogaśāstra, vol. I, p. 397, verse 95.

38. Aṅguttara-Nikāya, vol. II, tr. by F. L. Woodward, M.A., p. 89.

there was that of *Bahuśruta,* in between the degree of the Master and that of the Doctor. We have textual references to three distinct grades of this degree in a passage in he Kalpasūtra where we are told that the designation of Bahuśruta should be conferred on a versatile scholar, versed in different branches of knowledge, possessed of a keen interest in scientific pursuit, and a steady bent of mind, given to the habit of wandering from place to place in quest of knowledge.[39] This great academic distinction used to be bestowed on scholars who had already obtained the degree of Master of Arts and were prosecuting post-graduate studies below the requirements of a Doctorate. We have no knowledge of any Jaina monasteries conferring this degree on its students ; but we do know from I-Tsing that the University of Nālandā habitually conferred this academic honour on competent candidates. The following passage will bear out our contention : "A person who has studied so far as this (book), is said to have mastered the grammatical sceince, and may be compared to one who has learnt the Nine Classics and all the other authors of China. All the above mentioned books are studied by both priests and laymen ; if not, they cannot gain the fame of the well-informed (lit. much heard ; Bahuśruta, or 'knowing much of the Śruti.')"[40] Only brilliant scholars of exceptional capacity were allowed to take this course. It was a coveted degree demanded of a minister of a king preparatory to his appointment. "In the city of Viśāla there was a very heroic king named Nanda. He had a minister named Bahuśruta."[41]

The Doctorate :— Unlike the Master's degree the Doctorate is repeatedly mentioned in Jaina literature : Eminent Jaina church fathers like Hemacandra,[42] Śrīdeva,[43] Bappahaṭṭi,[44] Abhaya-

---

39. Sthavira Arya Bhadrabāhu Swami, Bṛhat Kalpa Sūtra, vol. I, p. 117, verse no. 400.

40. I-Tsing, A Record of Buddhist practices, tr. by T. Takakusu, p. 180.

41. Vikrama's Adventure, tr. by Franklin Edgerton, part I, p. 33.

42. Merutunga Ācārya, Prabandhacintāmaṇi, tr. by C. H. Tawney, M.A., p. 123.

43. *Ibid,* p. 98, 102.

44. *Ibid,* p. 201,.

sūri,[45] Jayamaṅgala,[46] Jayasena,[47] Śīlaguṇa,[48] Vijayasena,[49] and others were recepients of this great mark of honour. A typical Jaina Doctor such as Hemacandra was characterised by thirty-six marks. We read : "In as much as his mind was grounded in all the received religious treatises and Upaniṣads, and his body was adorned with the thirty-six good points of a Jaina doctor, his religious teacher formally conferred on him that dignity."[50] It is clear from the text that the requirements for the Doctor's degree in the Jaina monastery were of a comprehensive nature including a thorough knowledge of Jaina, as well as Vedic literatures and Arts. By the by, it is also evident that the candidates for Doctorate in the Jaina University were acquainted with the technique of research like their modern counterparts ; like them they too freely consulted the State records in order to prepare their theses. In support of our contention, the following lines may be quoted : "Then Kumudcandra, seated in a litter, and the Paṇdit Ratnaprabhā on foot, came into the Record office, to write down thesis and the counterstatement. Kumudcandra had his thesis taken down by the officials of the Record office."[51] That this high degree of scholarship required in the recepient of a Doctor's degree was almost universal is evident from the works of I-Tsing who gives us an idea of the standard that prevailed in the University of Nālandā. "The priests learn besides all the Vinaya works, and investigate Sūtras and Śāstras as well. They oppose the heretics as they would drive beasts (deer) in middle of a plain, and explain away disputations as boiling water melts frost. In this manner they became famous throughout Jambudvīpa (India), received respect above gods and men, and serving under the Buddha and promoting His doctrines. ....of such persons in every generation only one or two appear. ..These men could compose a work on the spot, whatever...subject was required—such men could commit to memory the contents of two volumes, having heard them only once."[52] From

---

45. Prabandhacintāmaṇi, p. 196.
46. *Ibid,* p. 93.
47. *Ibid,* p. 167.
48. *Ibid,* p.19.
49. *Ibid,* p. 157.
50. *Ibid,* p. 129.
51. *Ibid,* p. 100.
52. I-Tsing, A Record of Buddhist Practices, tr. by T. Takakusu, pp. 181-82.

two Arabian authorities of the ninth century A.D., we can gather that the pracice of conferring Doctorate was also in vogue in Ceylon. "The king of this land has laws which are the ground work of Religion and Government of the country. Here are Doctors, and Assemblies of learned men like those of the Hadiths among the Arabs. The Indians repair to these Assemblies and write down what they hear of the Lives of their prophets, and the various expositions of the Laws."[53]

It is definite that this great honour was never conferred on any student for the mere volume of his learning : originality and research were the most needful thing in a Doctor. The prospective Doctor had to look for truth in primary sources available in the State library or in the libraries of the monasteries. Kundakunda Ācārya composed his thesis in the State library.

In the Jaina as well as the Buddhist Universities, the scheme of work for a Doctor was very arduous. There were good many research scholars or prospective Doctors who became eminent authorities. In later times, one such typical scholar was Buddhaghoṣa himself. From the text it is clear that he looked for clarification and harmony of the truth of Buddhist philosophy. A good deal of elaborate study was needed for the purpose. In a word, researches in a Buddhist University required thorough criticism of a doctrine, test of its genuineness, synthesis and interpretation. "That which investigates impermanence, etc., is 'Search' (vicaya). 'Research' (pavicaya) shows increase by means of the prepositions. 'Search for doctrine' is that which investigates the doctrine of the Four Truths"[54] and we quote again : "In the exposition of 'investigation', the [kernel] of the word *cāra* expresses a going-about the object. This is the primary meaning. 'Investigation' indicates general scrutiny. The next terms with prefixes—anu-upa-vicāra indicate order and closeness in the investigation. Next, 'mental adjustment' indicates the mind being fitted to its object as an archer fixes his arrow to the bow-string, and 'examination' is either a sustained consideration, or the opposite—want-of-consideration (anu-

53. Ancient Account of India and China by two Mahommedan Travellers, tr. by Eusebius Reunando, pp. 83-84.

54. Buddhaghosa, The Expositor, vol. I, tr. by Maung Tin, M.A., p. 195.

pekkhatā, an-upekkhatā)."[55] This anticipates the spirit of thoroughness comprehensiveness and methodical elaborateness which are characteristics of a modern student engaged in the serious work of research. Quotations too were in vogue. For example, Rājaśekhara made quotations from Kālidāsa's Kumārasambhavam in the body of his work Kāvyamīmāṁsā.

Education in the Jaina monasteries, was a systematic, never-ending process practised by scholars from the cradle to the grave. Those Jaina monks were perennial students learning things spiritual and mental, through meditation, devotion and study.[56] John Dewey, the great American educationist, in a similar key characterized education as a continuous process. Precisely the same view was held by Manu on the one hand and Lord Buddha on the other. Manu required the Brahmin scholars to study the Vedas daily even after they have completed their courses of study in the technical sense. "Let him daily pour over those Institutes of science which soon give increase of wisdom, those which teach the acquisition of wealth, those which are beneficial (for other worldly concerns) and likewise over the Nigamas which explain the Veda."[57]

The Jaina monks, like their mediaeval counterparts in Europe besides studying used to copy manuscripts of valuable books in their cells. Thus they kept the torch of learning, burning. They used to go on preaching tours to different monasteries, to deliver extension lectures before large audience of both sexes. This was the practice common to both the Buddhists and the Jainas ; and Lord Mahāvīra, Lord Ṛṣabha, Dr. Hemacandra were all peripatetic teachers, delivering their messages to mankind for their permanent good.

We give below statistics on monastic education prepared from the pages of the Kalpasūtra. Even making allowance for exaggeration, we can get a fair idea of the diffusion of monastic education in India under the control of the Jaina fathers.

---

55. Buddhaghosa, The Expositor, vol. I, tr. by Maung Tin, M.A., p. 189.
56. The Uvāsagadasāo, tr. by A. F. Rudolf Höernle, Ph.D., p. 61, verse. 77.
57. Manu, tr. by G. Bühler, pp. 131-32, verse 19.

| | | | |
|---|---|---|---|
| I. Lord Ṛṣabha, the Kosalin had under him Ṛṣabhasena as head of the community of | 84,000 Śramaṇas | 305,000 lay votaries with Śreyāṃśa at their head. | 4750 sages who knew the 14 Pūrvas.<br>9000 sages who knew Avadhi knowledge.<br>(c) 20,000 Kevalins<br>(d) 20,600 sages who could transform themselves.<br>(e) 12,650 sages of vast intellect.<br>(f) 12,650 professors.<br>(g) 20,000 males who have reached perfection.<br>(h) 22,900 sages who reached their last birth. |
| II. Lord Ariṣṭanemi had under him Varadatta as head of a community of | 18,000 Śramaṇas | 169,000 lay votaries with Nanda at their head. | (a) 400 sages and<br>(b) 15,00 Kevalins who gained Avadhi knowledge.<br>(c) 15,00 sages who gained transform themselves.<br>(d) 1000 sages of vast intellect.<br>(e) 800 professors<br>(f) 16,00 sages in their last birth.<br>(g) 15,00 males who reached perfection. |
| III. Lord Pārsva had under him Āryadatta as the head of a community of | 16,000 Śramaṇas | 164,000 lay votaries with Suvrata at their head. | (a) 350 sages who knew 14 Pūrvas.<br>(b) 14,00 sages who gained Avadhi knowledge.<br>(c) 1000 Kevalins<br>(d) 11,00 sages who |

could transform themselves.

(e) 600 sages who acquired correct knowledge.

(f) 750 sages of vast intellect.

(g) 600 professors.

(h) 1200 sages who reached their last birth.[58]

IV. Lord Mahāvīra had directly under him

(A)

(a) 314 advanced disciples possesed of a wisdom next to perfection.

(b) 1300 disciples possessed of inductive knowledge.

(c) 700 disciples possessed of certain knowledge.

(d) 700 possessed of the power of assuming a different form

(e) 500 of large intellect

(f) 400 disputants

(g) 700 male disciples who after death obtained perfect liberation.

(h) 250 who obtained super-celectial mansion

(B)

The Lord had under him (1) Indrabhūti as head of the community of an excellent band of 14,000 male ascetics

(2) and Śaṅkhaśatakār as head of an excellent select band of 159,000 male lay adherents.[59]

---

58. Kalpasūtra, vol. I, p. 274, p. 278.

59. The Kalpa Sūtra And Nava Tatva, tr. by Rev. J. Stevenson, D.D., pp. 93-94.

# LECTURE V

## THE EDUCATION OF WOMEN—ECCLESIASTICAL.

The object of the present lecture is to offer to the audience an idea of education imparted to women as a preparation for ecclesiastical activities in Jaina India as far as it may be gathered from the available literature on the subject. It is clear that there were two distinct types of female education (1) The first type of education was imparted by nuns to prospective nuns in nunneries and to female lay votaries. (2) The second type of education was imparted in palace schools by lay teachers at any rate under the control of lay teachers with the secular object of training the students in the various duties of life relating to the family, the State and the rest.

Before we begin our theme proper, it may not be amiss to add a few words as to the social position and dignity of women in ancient India during the Hindu, the Buddhist and the Jaina periods. It is verily a fact that the woman in ancient India was not a mere drudge or a slave. The truth is the reverse. The popular supposition is sadly erroneous here. Even Manu while upholding the doctrine of her inferiority was for maintaining her dignity. "In childhood a female must be subject to her father ; in youth to her husband, when her lord is dead to her sons ; a woman must never be independent."[1] What is really astonishing is that this same authority recommended the appointment of females in the service of the State—a fact which will be clear from the following quotation. "For women employed in the royal service and for menial servants, let him fix a daily maintenance, in proportion to their position and to their work."[2] The climax is reached in the following extracts where we get an idea not only of the dignity but also of the apotheosis of women. "Women must be honoured and adorned by their fathers, brothers, husbands and brothers-in-law who desire (their own) welfare."[3] and we quote again "Where

1. Manu tr. by G. Bühler, p. 195, verse. 148.
2. *Ibid*, p. 236, verse. 125.
3. *Ibid*, p. 85, verse. 56.

women are honoured, there the gods are pleased ; but where they are not honoured, no sacred rite yields rewards."[4]

Let us now turn to the consideration of the position and dignity of women in the Buddhist India. Frankly speaking it was not a very elevated one. The Buddha was against admitting them into his Church and at last he admitted a few at the repeated request of his disciple, Ānanda. The Mahāprajāpati, Gotami, the Lord's step-mother was the first to be admitted into the order along with the five hundred Śākya princesses.[5]

The Buddha did not think women to be fit for practical affairs of life because of their inherent intellectual inferiority. His attitude on this point will be distinctly clear from the following words of the text. "Womenfolk are uncontrolled, Ānanda. Womenfolk are weak in wisdom, Ānanda. That is the reason, that is the cause why womenfolk do not sit in a court of justice, do not embark on business, do not reach the essence of the deed."[6] And again "It is impossible for a woman to be an emperor of the world ; but is possible for a man to be."[7] But once women were admitted into the Buddhist Order, women of all ranks—royal consorts,[8] females of aristocratic class,[9] widows,[10] cast off women,[11] curtezans,[12] and women of the lowest rank [13] in society were freely admitted by Lord Buddha into his cadet. He rehabilitated them through a course of religious education into his Order and made them fit for honourable profession of preaching and teaching. But it must be noted that within the limited sphere of ecclesiastical activities, the women once they were admitted were given a good deal of latitude.

---

4. Manu, tr. by G. Bühler, p. 85, verse. no. 56.
5. Vinaya Text Pitaka, part iii, tr. by T. W. Rhys Davids, p. 321, p. 327.
5a. Psalms of the Early Sisters, tr. by Mrs. Rhys Davids, p. 6, p. 7.
5b. Sadharma Pundarikā, tr. by H. Kern, p. 256.
6. Aṅguttara-Nikāya, vol. 11, p. 93.
7. Further Dialogue of Buddha, vol. ii, p. 191.
8. Psalms of the Early Sisters, pp. 81-82.
9. *Ibid,* p. 6, p. 48, p. 38.
10. *Ibid,* p. 62, p. 131.
11. Vinaya Text, vol. ii, pp. 105-106, p. 108.
11a. Psalms of the Early Sisters, p. 52.
12. *Ibid,* p. 96.
13. *Ibid,* p. 129, p. 131.

They were trained, encouraged and cheered up in their helpfully useful work of charity and popular benevolence to society.

The Jaina fathers were extremely sympathetic in their attitude to women and admitted them freely into their Order, no matter whether the candidates for admission were royal consorts, members of the aristocracy, and women belonging to the common run of society. There was not only equality but also ascendency and superiority of women to men in Jaina India,—a fact which is clear from the rather jarring note of protest from Dr. Hemacandra, the great Jaina father who warns men to beware of women and who emphasizes the dependency of men to women in all phases of life in infancy, in youth and in old age.[14]

Like the Buddhist nuns, their Jaina sisters held a subordinate position in the religious Order, though we do not have at our disposal, elaborate and systematic code regulating the inferior position of the Jaina nuns and their relationship. The nunnery of the Jainas was affiliated to the monastery and the Jaina nuns could almost rise to the position of a head of the community of nuns under an Arhat. Thus nuns Brāhmīsundarī,[15] Āryāyākinī,[16] Puṣpakūla,[17] and Candrabālā and Salasa Revati were heads of the community of Jaina nuns under the Arhats Ṛṣabha, Ariṣṭanemi, Pārśva and Mahāvīra respectively. We do not have any authentic evidence if the nuns ever reached the status of Ārhats or Siddhas. The geographical factors exerted a powerful influence on the selection of sites for the Jaina nunneries. We again see here the influence of location, topography, rivers, soil, flora, fauna, and transportation system in the selection of sites for the nunneries. The Jaina nunneries existed at Campā,[18] Mithilā,[19] Rājagṛha,[20] Śrāvasti,[21] Bāravai[22] (Dvārakā), and in Kammasadhamma in the Kuru kingdom.[23]

---

14. Hemacandra : Triṣaṣṭiśalākā-puruṣa-Caritra, vol. II, tr. by Helen M. Jhonson, Ph.D., p. 298.

15. Kalpasūtra, vol. I, tr. by Hermann Jacobi, p. 278.

16. *Ibid, Loc. Cit.* 17. *Ibid,* p. 274.

18. The Antagaḍadasāo And Anuttarovavāiyā Dasāo, tr. by L. D. Barnett, M.A., p. 98, p. 100. 19. *Ibid,* p. 24. 20. *Ibid,* p. 97.

21. The Kathākoṣa, tr. by C. H. Tawney, p. 13.

22. The Antagaḍadasāo And Anuttarovavāiyā Dasāo, p. 84.

23. Psalms of the Early Sisters, p. 57.

The inland bodies of water such as river and lake influenced the selection of the site for nunnery in Campaka. The city of Campaka, now an obscure village near modern Bhagalpur was an ancient city famous for its commercial, political and cultural activities through the ages. It is mentioned in the Mahābhārata as a holy place.[24] But the Jaina fathers ascribe its origin to Konikā or Ajātaśatru, the son of Śreṇika Bimbisāra who made it his capital. "Then, being unable to endure his sorrow for his father, he left Rājagṛha, and founded the new city, Champaka. This Konikā made the seat of his rule."[25]

According to Fa-Hian, the fifth century Chinese Buddhist pilgrim to India, it was located on the southern bank of the river Ganges.[26] Rhys Davids in the Dialogues of the Buddha claims its site on the east bank of the river Campaka.[27] The city was semi-circular in shape, and it was provided with all the facilities of the modern civilized life—buildings, excellent roads and the rest. The following quotation will bear us out. "In those days, at that time, there was a city named Campā. It was splendid, tranquil, and prosperous, city-folk and country-folk alike were happy there. It was thronged with population. Its field-bounds were turned up by hundreds and thousands of ploughshares, and displayed far-reaching pleasant dykes. ....It was surrounded by a wall bent in a curve like a bow, and decorated with cornices arranged in circles. Its bastions, rampart-paths, door-ways, gates and arches were lofty, its high-roads duly divided........It contained markets and bazaars, thronged with craftsmen, content and happy. It had open places, junctions of three, four or more roads, and markets for goods, adorned with diverse sorts of treasure.....Its highways were thronged with princes. It was crowded with number of fine horses, fiery elephants and troops of chariots, with palanquins and litters, and with cars and carriages. Its waters were brilliant with beds of lotuses whose buds were newly bursting into bloom, and it was fully decorated with fine white palaces."[28] Owing

24. Mahābhārata, vol. vi. edited by Haridas Siddhantavāgis, p. 780, verse no. 163.

25. Kathākoṣa, p. 178.

26. Fa-Hian, A Record of Buddhistic Kingdoms tr. by James Legge, M.A., LL.D., p. 100.

27. Dialogues of the Buddha, part, I, tr. by T. W. Rhys Davids, p. 144.

28. The Antagaḍadasāo And Anuttarovavāiyā Dasāo, pp. 1-2.

to its excellent situation in the front of a land naturally fertile, Campā flourished in commerce and trade ; and its citizens came to be noted for skill in agriculture, cattle-raising, etc. They became rich and prosperous and invested their money in contributing to the architectural excellence of the city and towards the course of religion in a variety of ways. As a rule, religion received great impetus from the public sympathy in the cities where people were placed above the common wants of life. Owing to the trade and commercial activities of the citizens of Campā they could afford to devote their leisure time and invest their surplus wealth for the cultural and religious activities of the city.

It is quite natural that the Jaina fathers will select site in such a city for nunneries where ladies of royal families readily joined the Jaina order. Thus in this city queen Kāli,[29] wife of Śreṇika Bimbisāra, and the step-mother of Kunie or Ajātaśatru was converted and she joined the Jaina nunnery where she studied the Laws of peace and the eleven scriptures. Here in this very city queen Sukāli[30] another wife of Śreṇika Bimbisāra and step-mother of prince Kunie joined the Jaina nunnery. Ajjā Candaṇā[31] was in charge of the nunnery at Campā.

The following nuns resided in the Jaina nunnery at Campā : Mahākāli,[32] Kaṇhā,[33] Sukaṇhā,[34] Mahākaṇhā, Virākaṇhā, Rāmakaṇha, Piuseṇākaṇhā,[36] and Mahāsenakanha.[37] Sivānandā, the wife of Ananda, a rich merchant at Vanijagrāma became the servant of Mahāvīra, the Jaina Ārhat when he visited the city.[38]

The city of Rājagṛha was a famous military city being encircled with five mountains.[39] This serves as an instance to show the religious

29. The Antagaḍadasāo And Anuttarovavāiyā Dasāo, p. 98.
30. *Ibid, Loc. Cit.*
31. *Ibid,* p. 98, p. 100.
32-34. *Ibid,* p. 101.
35. *Ibid,* p. 102.
36. *Ibid,* pp. 104-105
37. *Ibid,* p. 106.
38. The Uvāsagadasāo, vol. II, p. 41.
39a. Further Dialogues of the Buddha, vol. ii, tr. by Lord Chalmers, p. 192.
39b. The Romantic Legend of Śākya Buddha, tr. by Samuel Beal, p. 325.

and cultural activities of the military city encompassed with mountains. This famous capital of Magadha was an important centre of Jaina education being at once provided with a monastery and a nunnery, the latter being associated with the name of Nandā, the consort of Bimbisāra who embraced Jainism there and practised severe asceticism for a period of twenty years. Her was not a conversion due to a mere emotional impulse : she was thoroughly well-versed in the Scripture.[40] Here again a notable lady, Bhaddā by name, the daughter of the king's treasury entered the ascetic order after putting an end to the life of her criminal husband in the Robber's cliff at Rājagṛha. There is a romantic flavour mixed up with the devotion in the whole story, which may be described as follows : She learnt the sacred text of the Nigaṇṭhas in the local nunnery and left Rājagṛha for further knowledge receiving instruction from different wisemen at different places. When she found herself competent she challenged the captain of the Norm presumably Sāriputra and at Śrāvastī she entered into a debate with the Śākyan reclus and assailed him with questions after questions all of which he answered with satisfaction. Then Sāriputra took his turn and when Bhādda failed to answer his question she embraced Buddhism.[41] Here we find a wonderful specimen of female scholarship in ancient India comparable to that of Gārgī who challenged the sages in the field of scholarship. The conversion of the girl Bhuya is equally interesting throwing a flood of light on the excellence of female education in ancient India. "Then the girl Bhuya, surrounded by her retinue, went, right through the midst of the city of Rājagṛha, to the temple Guṇaśilā ; and having gone there....she got out of the chariot meant for religious journeys, and surrounded by the circle of the maidservants she went to her Lord Pārswa who is greatly renowned in the world and having circumambulated him three times, waited upon him.

"The Lord Pārswa, who is greatly renowned in the world, delivered to that girl Bhuya and to the great assembly the religious instruction. Having heard and bestowed to it she was greatly delighted, and saluted and bowed down to him, and having done so, she spoke thus to him.

---

40. The Antagaḍadasāo And Anuttarovavāiyā Dasāo, p. 97.
41. Psalams of The Early Sisters, pp. 64-66.

'I believe, venerable sir, in the Doctrine of the Nigganthas (and so forth, down to) I have stood for that............'

"She went to her parents, and having folded her hands she asked their permission exactly as in the case of Jamali in Bhagavatisūtra.... after dinner....he consented to the renunciation of his daughter."[42] Then followed the formal admission of Bhuya into the Order. "Then that girl Bhuya, being thus spoken to by the Lord Pārswa and becoming greatly delighted ....in the presence of Pupphachula nuns (and so forth, down to) become a self-restrained nun."[43] As in the Jaina monasteries it was also customary for the nuns to study regularly, "and wherever she spread her bed or seat for study she first of all sprinkled that place with water."[44] The case of Bhuya suggests two fundamental facts : (1) First, like the Buddhist monastery co-education was practised in the Jaina monastery where sermon could be attended by the males and the females alike, and (2) Second, vehicles played an important role in the dissemination of Jaina culture and faith among the people.

Benares, the sacred city was an abode of cosmopolitan culture. Here the followers of different and even conflicting creeds met together and lived in a spirit of amity and concord. The Hindus, the Buddhists and the Jains were there. The Jainas had their monasteries and nunneries in this sacred city flourishing side by side wiith the temples of the Hindus and the Vihāras of the Buddhists. We learn that the Suvaya nuns living at Benares used to beg their food from all classes of citizens —the high, the middle and the poor. The nun Soma studied the eleven Aṅgas such as Sāmaiya and others under the Suvaya nuns.[45]

Jaina nunneries existed at Sāketapura, Kammasadhamma in Kuru kingdom, Bāravaī (Dvārakā), Polāspura, and at other centres.

The Jaina nunneries served as places of relief and shelter to many a distressed lady in the high rank of life. Thus it is on record that a widowed princess of a local royal household sought shelter in the nunnery of Śrāvastī against the evil design of her brother-in-law, the king of Sāketapura.[46]

---

42. The Niryāvaliyāo, edited by A. S. Gopani, M.A., pp. 118-120, 1531156.
43. *Ibid*, pp. 121-122, 159.
44. *Ibid*, pp. 118-120.
45. *Ibid*, pp.118-120, 153-156.
46. Kathākoṣa, p. 13.

The volume, the magnitude as well as the excellence of culture attained by womanhood in Jaina India can be gathered even from the fragmentary evidence we have at our disposal. We have already cited an example of female scholarship of sterling merit in Jaina India. The arrangement for instructions in philosophy and theology given to female students in Jaina nunneries was as perfect as possible. We may add a few more examples to this glorious list. Nanduttarā was another Jaina nun to challenge Moggallāna, another apostle of Lord Buddha. She came of a Brahmin family of Kammasadhamma in the kingdom of Kuru. Having learnt the arts and sciences of her caste she joined the Jaina order. She gradually came to be known as a famous orator in which she must have acquired skill in the Jaina nunnery. In the debate with Moggallāna she was defeated and embraced Buddhism.[47]

There was Bāravaī or Dvārakā celebarted in the Mahābhārata and the Purāṇas as the capital of Lord Kṛṣṇa. According to Jaina literature the city was twelve *yojanas* in length and nine *yojanas* in dimensions. The city is located on the extreme north-western periphery of Guzerat and is on the immediate vicinity of the coast of Arabian sea. It had on its north-eastern side Revayae (modern Girnar), the mountain full of floras and faunas of diverse kinds.[48]

Queen Paumāvai of Bāravaī was admitted into the Jaina order by saint Ariṭṭhaṇemi. She plucked her own hair and was handed over to the nun Yakkhiṇī for training in the laws of peace and in eleven scriptures. She led the life of a nun for full twenty years and then starved herself to death.[49]

Queen Gori, consort to Kaṇhe Vasudeva, king of Bāravaī also renounced the world and joined the Jaina order.[50] In this city princess Mūlasiri, wife of prince Sambe, son of king Kaṇhe renounced the world and joined the Jaina order.[51] These significant and glorious examples emphatically illustrate the magnitude of the influnece of Jainism in the field of spiritual culture : Jainism affected the very springs of life

47. Psalms of The Early Sisters, p. 57.
48. The Antagaḍadasāo And Anuttarovavāiyā Dasāo, pp. 12-13.
49. *Ibid*, p. 84.
50. *Ibid*, Loc. Cit.
51. *Ibid*, Loc. Cit.

to the extent of persuading the members of the softer sex to give up a life of luxury and ease in favour of a life of stern asceticism because the latter leads to emancipation. Aggimittā was converted in the presence of Lord Mahāvīra in the Sahassambavaṇa garden in the town of Polāśpura.[52]

We do not have detailed account regarding the Jaina nunneries in the different parts of India. Happily for us the Kalpasūtra has recorded statistical account of the activities of Brāhmīsundarī, Āryāyākṣini, Puṣpakūlā and Candrabālā and Salasā Revati the five nuns under the leadership of Ārhat Ṛṣabha, Ariṣṭanemi, Pārśva and Mahāvīra respectively. Even making allowance for exaggeration if any, we can safely conclude from the statistical account given below that the nuns were very numerous numbering 378,000 ; and 12,170,00 female votaries and 45,000 female disciples who had reached perfection. We give below the statistical table prepared from the pages of Kalpasūtra :—[53]

| | (1) | (2) | (3) |
|---|---|---|---|
| (I) The Arhat Ṛṣabha, the Kosalian had under him nun Brāhmīsundarī as head of the community of | 300,000 nuns | 554,000 female lay votaries with Subhadra at their head | 40,000 female disciples who had reached perfection. |
| (II) Arahat Ariṣṭanemi had under him nun Ārya Yakṣini as head of the community of | 40,000 nuns | 336,000 female lay votaries with Mahāsuvrata at their head | 3,000 female disciples who had reached perfection. |
| (III) Arhat Pārsva had under him nun Puṣpakula as head of the community of | 38,000 nuns | 327,000 female lay votaries with Sunandā at their head | 2,000 female disciples who reached perfection. |

52. Uvāsagadasāo, vol. iii, p. 140, para II.
53. Kalpasūtra, vol. I, tr. by Hermann Jacobi, p. 284.

| | |
|---|---|
| (IV) Lord Mahāvīra had under him nun | |
| 1) Chandrabala as head of a community of | a select band of 36,00 female ascetics. |
| 2) And nun Salasā Revati as head of a community of | an excellent select band of 318,000 female lay adherents.[54] |

The Lord Mahāvīra himself had directly under him 14 females who obtained perfect liberation on death.

We learn from Hemacandra's Trisaṣtiśalākāpuruṣacaritra that 300, 000 nuns and 554,000 lay women existed in India.[55] From the statistical table cited above we get a glimpse of the tremendously effective type of spiritual culture affecting the female life in Jaina India—a glorious movement of education of which any age or country in the world could be or should be proud.

---

54. The Kalapasutra And Nava Tattva, tr. by Rev. J. Stevenson, D.D., pp. 93-94.

55. Trisaṣtiśalākāpurusacaritra, vol. I, p. 358.

# LECTURE VI

## EDUCATION OF WOMEN—LAY.

In this lecture we propose to discuss the education of female lay scholars imparted outside the pale of the Jaina nunneries for secular purposes. The Family, the State and the School were vitally interested in the education of the lay scholars. It was universally prevalent, intensely practical having a sound psychological basis. The nuns who joined the Jaina Order were women of mature age as a rule ; and consequently, they were thoroughly fit for their task, being well versed both in secular and sacred learning. There was a sound knowledge of child and adolescent psychology in the background of the process of education they imparted to their students. The physical and mental growth of the child is gradual and not sudden. The following quotation will give us an idea of their knowledge of child-psychology. "Twins Yaśasvin and Surūpā were born. Having the (same) joints, figure and colour (as their parents), a little shorter lived, they gradually attained growth, like strength and intellect. . . .together they gradually grew up like intellect and vigour."[1] The characteristics of physically growing child are restlessness, exhuberance of energy, playfulness and hardness. In brief they are fond of sense and motor activities and are restless owing to the urge of inner energy. During this period their emotions of love, and anger are also manifested. "These grew up gradually, playing here and there, very strong, very energetic, like young elephants on the Vindhya Mountains.

"The passions, anger, etc., of the twins appeared like grains of lac on asvattha trees, gradually, gradually."[2] Though the physical, emotional and mental traits are gradually manifested in the growing child these continue to grow unmitigated in an ideal child born of ideal parentage.

---

1. Hemacandra : Triṣaṣṭiśalākā-puruṣa-Caritra, vol. II, tr. by Helen M. Johnson, Ph.D., pp. 98-99.

2. *Ibid*, p. 148.

An elaborate and an almost astonishingly modern description of the eight stages of the human life is given in the Uvāsagadasão. There are, according to this Aṅga eight stages of development altogether, each logically following the other. The first stage contains seven days commencing from the birth of the child. This is a period of pure inactivity, during which the child does not respond to outside stimuli and all its senses are totally inactive. The second stage is the stage of playful activities during which the child cries, laughs and coughs; in a word responds to outside stimuli. It is a period of restlessness and motion. This is followed by the third stage, the stage of experiment on the part of the child—through the help of its parents or others. The fourth stage is the stage of unaided walk—the stage of independent motion on the part of the child. Then follows the fifth stage which is associated with the fitness of the body and the ripeness of the mind—a stage of life when the child is pre-eminently fit to learn the acts. The following quotation supports our statement. "Eight stages of man (puriṣa-bhumiya) he designated the following eight developmental periods of man : the dull-stage, the playful-stage, the experimental-stage, the erect--stage, the learning-stage, the ascetic-stage, the Jina-stage, and the prostrate-stage. What he means is this : beginning with the day of birth, for (a period) of seven days, till they come out of a condition of mental obstruction, (living) beings are dull (manda) or semi-conscious, (momuha). This he calls 'the dull-stage' (manda-bhumi). Afterwards those that have arrived (in the present birth) from a state of torment (in a previous existence) prepetually cry and scream ; while those that have come from a state of happiness laugh in the perpetual recollection of it. This he calls the 'playful-stage' (khiḍḍa-bhumi), Then when they attempt to walk along on the ground, holding on the hands or legs of their parents or to a bed or stool, that he calls the "experimental-stage" (vimamsabhumi). The time when they are fully able to walk on their feet, he calls 'the erect-stage' (ujugata-bhumi). The time when they are made to learn the arts, he calls 'the learning-stage' (sekhā-bhumi). The time, when leaving their houses, they devote themselves to a life of ascetic mendicancy, he calls the 'ascetic-stage' (Samana-bhumi). The time when, after a continuous course of ascetic practices, they attain perfect knowledge, he calls 'the Jina-stage' (Jina-bhumi). When a mendicant, becoming a prostrate Jina, no longer speaks (i.e., begs) anything. showing thereby that he has become an ascetic who is passed all wants, that he calls 'the prostrate stage.' (punna-bhumi)."[3]

From the above description it is quite clear that the Jaina theorists in the field of education had a sound, profound, and scientific knowledge of child psychology and adult psychology without which it is impossible to frame a scheme of education. Education, after all, is for man ; and not man for education. A further light is thrown on this aspect of the question in a quotation inserted below from Hemacandra on the physical growth of an aristocratic lady. "He had a wife, named Laksmana, who had all the favourable marks, surpassing the moon in fascinating beauty of face. Though possessing a body which was an unequalled stream of loveliness, she rained only nectar with her eye and speech. Walking very slowly, she made mellows grow at every step with her feet, as it were. Her brow and gait were curved, but her mind was not crooked ; her waist was small, but not the wealth of her intelligence. The important virtue of proper behaviour adorned like a general, her entire army of virtue surpassing everything."[4] It is a common knowledge that adolescent girls are notorious for wildness, looseness, desire for promiscuous company and sexual eccentricities. These are universal prevailing in all the ages, in countries, and in all stages of culture ; and the ancient India was not exception to the rule. We read in the Prabandhakoṣa, vol. I, the story of Varudatta, the daughter of a serpent king indulging in youthful pranks with fourteen mates of her own age.[5] Taking into account the physical, emotional and mental traits of the females from their birth to adolescence, it was quite natural for them to attend the art School in their girlhood to early adolescence. For the curricula of the art-Schools were of such nature as to fit these well into their physical, emotional and mental traits. Naturally the Jaina fathers prescribed the art education for the girls in their girlhood instead of Vedic education. The Vedic education was to be superimposed upon the art or primary and secondary education.

3. The Uvāsagadasāo, vol. ii, tr. by A. F. Rudolf Höernle, p. 23.
4. Triṣaṣṭiśalākā-puruṣa-Caritra, vol. II, pp. 315-316.
5. Rājeśekhara Sūri, Prabandhakoṣa, vol. I, p. 87.

The course of studies prescribed for females were eminently practical and physiologically sound, having a special eye to the mental aptitude of the students and their prospects in the future as members of the State, of the Church, of the School or of the Family. It may be added that music was also included in the scheme of studies and those who had special aptitude for it specialized in it. "Gandharvadatta has been brought up in the city of Gandharvas. She is skilled in all the Arts but more especially in music....."

"Let there be at Campa a musical competition every six months. At it Gandharvadatta will sing the nārāyaṇastuti."[6]

Specialization was in vogue very much as it is to-day. Students pursued a thorough study in a particular branch of knowledge which was quite in harmony with their practical bents of mind ; some specialized in painting, some in dancing, others in singing and so forth. This is typically illustrated by the story of the princess Śrīmatī whose sorrows were soothed by her learned and skilful nurse by means of depicting the story of her life-story on a piece of canvass. Associated with the knowledge of painting was the knowledge of geography and of city, transportation-system and others. The story referred to may be given in the following words. "One day Śrīmatī had gone to a pleasure-garden, and her nurse, named Paṇḍita, seized a favourable opportunity and spoke to her privately..... When I know your grief, I shall proceed to the business of curing it............She then told Paṇḍita an exact account of her former life, like a man making confession to a good guru. Having represented Śrīmatī's story on a canvas by pictures, Panditā, learned in strategy, went quickly to display it outside."[7] The same story is repeated in the Mahāpurāṇa by Puṣpadanta, a tenth century writer. He represented Śrīmatī drawing herself the portrait of Lalitāṅga, her lover on a piece of canvas and handed it over to her nurse to find out the whereabouts of her lover.[8] An inter-

---

p. 131.

6. Professor Fiślix Lacôte, Essay on the Guṇadhya and the Bṛhat Kathā,

7. Triṣaṣṭiśalākā-puruṣa-Caritra, vol. II, p. 60.

8. Puṣpadanta, Mahāpurāṇa, vol. I, edited by Dr. P. L. Vaidya, chap. 22, verse 21.

esting story of romantic import similar to the story of Paṇḍitā is related by another authority, Haribhadra Sūri in his Samāricca Kahā. Here we are all told how the nurse Madanalekhā relieved the mind of her ward, princess Kusumāvali by painting a picture of her mind on a canvas. The story is given in the following words. "Then Medanalekhā brought the painting board with a brush and said to Kusumāvali : 'My lady, the prince is fond of painting; so my lady paints here a female swan, who is separated from her proper partner and is therefore anxious to see him.' Then understanding the opinion of Madanalekhā she smiled a little and painted the female swan as was advised. Madanalekhā also wrote upon it the Dwipadikhanda suggesting the condition of Kusumāvali.[9] Thus Hemacandra, Puṣpadanta, and Haribhadra Sūri all advocated the story of painting for young adolescent girls or ladies for expressing adequately and concretely their life-stories and emotions such as love so predominant in them in their first bloom. Thus painting for them has practical utility of winning the hearts of their lover and in solving the adolescent problem of choosing and winning life's companion. Rightly enough music and painting constituted important items of liberal education in those days of yore. They provided men and women not only with a source of innocent recreation, but also with a stimulus to the development of imagination without which no culture can be perfect. Over and above there was also an element of utility in the matter of matrimony.

As we noticed before sense and motor activities are predominant in girlhood and in adolescence owing to surplus energy. Dancing, games and physical education courses of the Art School were of immense value in satisfying the physical needs of the young girls and early adolescents. Naturally, organized games and physical exercises formed an item of their courses of training in the art-School. The princess utilized their skill in physical exercises, games and in dancing in the proper use of their pastimes, recreation and in physical exercise. We quote below to support our statement. "So was the harem of princess ; who were averse from the ball-play ; who gave up the activities of painting ; who stopped all music and dance."[10]

9. Haribhadra Sūri, Samarâicca-Kahā, tr. by M. C. Modi, M.A., LL.B., p. 80.
10. *Ibid*, p. 23.

A few gifted scholars alone could master the encyclopaedic courses in the art-school which according to Jaina fathers are seventy-two[11] and according to the Brahmins sixty-four.[12] These courses comprising 3 R's, languages, fine Arts : music, painting, pictography, dancing, physical exercises such as games, military exercises, sciences such as astrology, astronomy and other courses were pursued by female-students gradually as they developed physically, mentally and emotionally as they grew in years. Hence the courses in the Art or Vernacular Schools were properly adjusted to the needs of the growing female-scholars. The Jaina fathers also included the Vedas and the Vedāṅgas in the curricula of the Art School. The following paragraphs from the Kathākoṣa will substantiate the above statement. "In the country Vidrabha, there was a city named Kuṇḍinapura. In it was a king, by name Bhimaratha. He had a wife Pushpadanti. As they were living together in loving union, they had a daughter born to them. . . .the child was called Devadanti. She grew every day like a digit of the moon in the white fortnight. In due course she was sent to a teacher of accomplishments, to acquire knowledge, and she gradually became clever in all learning."[13] Education was by no means a monopoly of the Brahmins : Kṣatriya and Vaiśya females too enjoined the blessings of higher learning and culture. We have evidence of higher education on the part of a girl belonging to the Vaiśya class who by a single scribal alteration converted a man doomed to death by her father into her husband. There is a romantic and poetic flavour about the whole story which is given below. "In the meantime the daughter of that merchant, Vishā by name, came there to worship the God of love. She saw Damanaka with his broad eyes and broad chest ; and while she was looking at him, her eye fell on her father's letter, she took it from the end of his stick and read it. It ran as follows : 'Health and prosperity, Sāgarapota from the cattle-farm lovingly embraces Samudragupta, and tells him what is to be done'.

'Before he has time to wash his feet, you must immediately bestow on this man Viṣa (poison) and so make my heart free from the thorn of pain.'

---

11a. Aṇuogadāra, p. 30.

11b. Prabandhakoṣa, vol. I, p. 27.

12. Lalitavistara, tr. by Dr. Rajendra Lal Mitra, pp. 186-188.

13. The Kathākoṣa, tr. by C. H. Tawney, M.A., p. 195.

She thought : 'No doubt my father has found here a bride-groom fit for me ; as for the marriage having to be performed this very day, it means that to-day is an auspicious day, so the marriage must take place to-day. As for the order that Visha is to be given, in his eagerness he has written an anusvara instead of the long a ' so I will put it right, Having thus reflected, she took some collyrium from her eyes and made the letter á instead of a dot ; and sealing the letter up again, she left it as it was and went home."[14] The Art-School was attended not only by the Kṣatriya and the Vaiśya girls, but also by their Brahmin sisters prior to their learning the Vedic sciences. Thus it proves clearly that even in Buddhist period it became the fashion among the Brahmins especially the girls to attend the vernacular schools before receiving instruction in the Vedic sciences. "She, too, faring in the past as the fore mentioned Sisters, was, in this Buddha age, born in the kingdom of the Kurus at the town of Kammasadamma, in a Brahmin family. And when she had learnt from some of them their Arts and sciences, she entered the order of the Niganṭhas."[15]

We have also authoritative evidence in the Skandapurāṇa supporting the views that a Brahmin girl, daughter of Hariswami of Benares joined the art-school where she excelled in fine arts.[16] The universal popularity of dancing and music is clearly stressed in the Agnipurāṇa which speaks highly of the teacher of Fine Arts and assigns him a residence in the heaven.[17]

Education of all grades from the primary to the higher was not denied even to the menials in society during the Jaina period of which we have evidence in the Prabandhacintāmaṇi. The females in the higher institutions of learning received secular education. We learn from the Prabandhakoṣa, vol. I, that Madanamanjari, the daughter of king Kuntibhoja of Vijayapura was versed in the higher branches of learning and she wrote from behind the screen five hundred ślokas of a book composed by a Digambara saint. This instance proves that the princess was competent enough to be engaged even as a scribe. "राज्ञोक्तम्-

14. Kathākoṣa, p. 172.
15. Psalms of the Early Sisters, p. 57.
16. Skandhapurāna, 4th canto, edited by Kālikṛṣṇa Mandal, p. 729.
17. Agnipurānam, edited by Pandit Pañchānan Tarkaratna, p. 402, verse 54.

अस्मत्पुत्री मदनमञ्जरी नाम लिखिष्यति जवनिकान्तरिता सती। दिगम्बरेण ग्रन्थः कर्त्तुमारेभे। राजपुत्री पत्रशतीं लिखति।'[18] Women were also versed in varied languages and costume of different countries as the following quotation shows. "नानादेशवेश भाषाविचक्षणाः शशाङ्कमुखीर्विशालनितम्बस्थलास्तारुण्यपुण्यावयवाः स्त्री।"[19]

Even a widow of tender age though very wise and well versed in all the śaṣtras and skillful in the art of speech is also acquainted with the domestic work. Such a learned window not only keeps herself busy with house-work but also causes others to be engaged in such a work. 'आभडस्य च चाम्पलदेनाम्नी वालविधवा वाग्मिनी उचितज्ञा सर्वशास्त्रविदुरा तनया गृहव्यापारान् करोति कारयति।"[20]

We already cited examples of educated ladies seeking employment in royal households. We may now refer to an instance of an old female cook receiving the blessing of culture. The case is given in the following authoritative words. "When she persisted in this endeavour, there was produced in her intellectual ability ; and so, after she had to a certain extent studied the three Vedas, the Raghuvaṁca, the Kāmaśāstra of Vātsyāyana, and the writings of Cāṇakya on morals and the principles of Government, she went with her daughter, named Vijayā, who was in her fresh youth and learned."[21]

During the period of the ascendency of the Jainas in India, it is patent that the Family, the Church, the School and the State served as powerful agents for the spread of education among women. We are told in the Mahāpurāṇa how Sundarī, a princess learnt various Arts from Bharata, the son of king Ṛṣabha. Jaina literature does not explicitly refer to the state of education for the lay females in the nunneries but it does so implicitly ; and we have an incidental reference to princess Gangāsenā of Gangapura receiving religious instructions from Chandrayasas a local abbess.[22]

We are quite in the dark about the School-buildings and

---

18. Rājaśekhara Sūri, Prabandhakoṣa, vol. I, p. 64.
19. *Ibid*, p. 92.
20. *Ibid*, p. 100.
21. Prabandhacintāmaṇi, p. 63.
22. Kathākoṣa, p. 116.

equipment of the art-school for the girls. We have references to the use of writing-tablet in the art-school in the Lalitavistara,[23] the Jātakas,[24] Kālidāsa's Raghuvaṃsa[25] and in Alberuni's India,[26] vol. I. We also learn from the Prabandhacintamaṇi the use of notice-board and white chalk in writing purposes.[27]

That the diploma of Paṇḍitā used to be conferred upon the competent lady-alumni of the higher institutions of learning is evident from the word "Paṇḍita" being prefixed to the names of some of the females. Besides such Paṇḍita could compose poems or make up the lost portion of a manuscript on the spot which even her learned father could not recover. We quote below in support of the above statement. "While the Paṇḍita was reproaching him in these words, king Bhoja burnt that original draft in the blazing fire. Then the Paṇḍit was doubly dispirited and doubly crest-fallen, and he flung himself down on an old couch in the back part of his palace, and lay there sighing deeply. His daughter Bālapaṇḍitā roused him from his stupor with loving attention and made him bathe and eat and drink, and then remembering the first half of the Tilakamañjari from having seen the writing of the first draft of it, she wrote it out, and the second half she composed anew, and so completed the book."[28]

Co-education seems to have prevailed in the Jaina Art-schools as well as in the monasteries. The case of Bhuya to which reference has already been made is a typical instance to the point : she attended extension lectures along with males at the Gūṇaṣila monastery at Rājagṛha. The extension lectures of the monasteries, it appears, used to be attended by audience of both sexes. The abode of Kaṇva, the god-father of Śakuntalā described in the immortal drama of Kālidāsa seems to have been an ideal co-educational hermitage. This co-education was of a very restricted type ; but it was nevertheless there. From Kālidāsa's Vikramorvasī and Śakuntalā we get an idea of Kālidāsa's

---

23. Kathākośa, p. 116.
24. Lalitavistara, p. 182.
25. Jātaka's, vol. I, tr. by Chalmars, p. 275.
26. Kālidāsa's Raghuvaṁsa, canto xviii.
27. Alburini's India, vol. I, tr. by D. E. C. Sachau, vol. I. p. 182.
28. Prabandhacintāmaṇi. p. 36.
29. *Ibid,* p. 61.

views regarding the educational activities of the hermitage. The hermitage was a co-educational institution admitting males and females where they received both theoretical and practical education in a spiritual atmosphere to fit them for their future vocations.

From the above we are in a position to conclude that co-education was in vogue in ancient India ; and among others the Jaina educationists effectively helped it through their various agencies of education : specialism was incessantly praised in the field of education ; and what is really astonishing, physical and even military training were given to women. It is implied in the Jaina literature as the whole range of seventy-two Arts were prescribed for the females. Females were not debarred by the Jaina fathers from receiving the same kind of education with the males. The Jainas recognized the equality of the two sexes. Only individual interests, aptitudes, temperaments, tastes and needs determined the type of education to be pursued by any student. Needs of society, State and industry also were taken into account. The same view was advocated by Rājaśekhara in his Kāvyamimaṁsā which was referred to in our introductory remark. The educated women filled important positions in the family, the school, or higher institutions of learning, in the church or nunnery and in the State. Briefly speaking they were not burden to society but were its active members and did much for the cultural, mental, moral and social upheaval of the country in ancient and mediaeval India and their education was vitally related to the realities of life. Thus we get an edifying sketch of female education prevalent in ancient India among the Jainas—a sketch which may be read with interest and profit even by moderns of our scientific age. Here we get a graphic illustrations of sound theories of education on elaborately comprehensive scale. All honour to our venerable ancesters who could think so much and do so much in those hoary days of antiquity.

# LECTURE VII

## THE EDUCATION OF THE PRINCES.

In a truly platonic spirit as it were the ancient and mediaeval rulers of India approached the problem of the education of the future guardians of the States or more explicity the princes and the princesses on whom the destiny of the country mainly depended, in a spirit of conformity with scientific principles, all the more so in an aristocratically and autocratically governed States of India. Those autocratic rulers of India were in most cases themselves highly cultured and rightly enough they appreciated the benefit of learning and patronised it with judicious liberality. But education like charity begins at home ; and they began by bestowing an elaborate attention to the education of their children from the cradle or more exactly from the embryonic stage in the womb. The future mother was well fed, well provided with light, refreshment, recreation, and an atmosphere favourable to the health of the foetus. This reveals both an insight and foresight and a true understanding of the mature and the magnitude of the problem of education in the true sense of the term. From a passage quoted below we can form an unmistakable idea of the thorough knowledge of the prenatal conditions that must be fulfilled by an ideal mother. Thus the consort of Andhaga-Vaṇhi, king of Bāravaī took special care during her pregnancy stage. "She nourished herself according to place and time with substances neither to chill nor too hot, nor too acrid, nor too pungent. nor too astringent, nor too sour, nor too sweet, but pleasant in seasonable use, with food, covering, perfumes, and garlands, such as were good for the unborn babe, moderate, wholesome, nutritious for the unborn babe, using special and soft beds and couches, staying in pleasantly retired and agreeable places of abode, her longings excellent, her longings fulfilled, duly honoured, entirelly gratified, dispelled, and removed, free from sickness, sorrow, delusion, dread, and terror, she comfortably carried unborn babe. Then, after the passing of nine months and seven and a half days and nights, queen Dharini bore a baby delicate of hands and feet, his body perfect and in no wise lacking in its five organs of sense, excellent in the marks of distinction and token.... sweet of aspect as the moon, lovely and pleasant to, behold a goodly form."[1]

The Jaina fathers were far ahead of the modern psychologists in their advocacy of the gradual growth of the human organism from the embryonic stage to its maximum period of growth in the adult period. "Then the embryo grew secretly day by day in lady Siddhartha's womb, like the seed-vessel in the calyx of a lotus."[2] We have already noticed, in connection with our sixth lecture the eight stages of life which pertain to both sexes. We may further note that of these, the first five stages of development come within the purview of the pre-school stage which may broadly be distinguished into two : (1) there is the stage of inactivity followed by (2) the stage of response to external stimuli. There is a Buddhist legend about a Brahmin illus trating the period.[3] Dr. Fergusson refers to a relevant portrait in the following words. "In the chamber on the right or east side of the sanctuary, are sculptured a pair of partly sitting figures, both with rich head-dresses : the woman holds a child on her knee, apparently amusing it with a toy held in her right hand ; to the right and left of them are female slaves with chauries, whilst, one beholds a parrot and a fruit. Below are eleven small figures, some of them making rams butt, others wrestling, and some playing on musical instrument for the child's amusement. This is probably intended to represent the infancy of Buddha nursed by his mother Māyādevī (or Mahāprajāpati) with a peculiar headdress, who sit by his father, Śuddhodana."[4] This practice of amusing the infants with ball and musical performances by expert ladies resemble very well the modern kindergarten ideals in ancient India. In the third stage of development, the young child learns to walk with the aid of the nurse. The point was stressed by Kālidāsa in his Raghuvaṃśa where young Raghu is described as learn-

1. The Antagaḍadasāo And Aṇuttarovavāiya-dasāo, tr. by L. D. Barnett, pp. 25-26.

2. Hemacandra : Triṣaṣṭiśalākā-puruṣa-Caritra, vol. ii, tr. by Helen M. Johnson, Ph.D., p. 258.

3. The Romantic Legend of Sākya Buddha, tr. by Samuel Beal, p. 316.

4. James Fergusson, D.C.L. and James Burgess, The Cave Temples of India, p. 333-334.

ing to walk and utter half hazard way from the nurse or demi-mother by holding her finger.[5] In the fourth stage it can stand on its own legs and walk about unassisted. The second and third and fourth stages of development from infancy to childhood is described in the Antagaḍadasāo in connection with the rearing of Lord Gotama, prince of Bāravaī (Dvaravatī) in his infancy as follows. "Now little Goyama was attended by five nurses to wit, a wet-nurse, (a2-bath-nurse, a tiring-nurse, a lap-nurse, and a play-nurse-also by many—women of diverse lands, in foreign garb. .skilful and accomplished, well-trained. Surrounded by this goodly throng of slave-girls and band of maids, encompassed by eunuchs, messengers, and chamberlains, he was passed from hand to hand, he enjoyed breast after breast, he was danced about, sung to, caressed, embraced, hugged, praised, kissed, made to walk upon delightful jewelled floors, and so grew in comfort."[6]

The fourth stage (ujugatabhūmi)[7] is characterized by restlessness peculiar to childhood due to sense and motor activities brought about by surplus inner energy. During this period they jump, and run about, and are fond of birds and butterflies of variegated colours. The children have recourse to various tricks to elude the vigilance of their nurses and make them worried by their wild demeanour. In brief childhood is characterized by physical activities and restlessness. "Running about rapidly as they liked, they tired out their nurses—running after them. Strength is a quality of the noble. The royal boys, the vāyukumarakas in speed, caught birds, pleasure-parrots, peacocks, etc. By various kinds of flattery, the nurses halted the boys in their course as they wandered at pleasure."[8] We quote again "getting down repeatedly from their laps with the restlessness usual to children, tricking his nurses again and again, the Lord passed his childhood, playing in various games."[9]

---

5a. Kālidāsa's Raghuvaṁsam, canto I, verse no. 25.

5b. D. C. Das Gupta's Educational Ideas in Kālidāsa's India, P. B. March, 1942.

6. The Antagaḍadasāo And Aṇuttarovavāiya-dasāo, pp. 28-29.

7. B. M. Barua's A History of per-Buddhistic Indian Philosophy, pt. III—Philosophy of Maskarin Gośāla.

8. Triṣaṣṭiśalākā-puruṣa-Caritra, vol. II, Ph.D., p. 67.

9. *Ibid*, p. 307.

Thus infancy and childhood were passed in the company of the educated and skilful nurses amidst physical and motor activities and appropriate arrangements were made for organized games and informal education under their care, and toys of diverse kinds were provided them to play with. Group activities were encouraged where sociability and national manners and etiquette and mother tongue were taught to them by nurse. Thus to use Comenius' term in the "School of infancy" the children learn in an informal way from their nurse—the upamātā useful information quite appropriate to their physical and mental growth. In the fifth stage (sekhā-bhumi) at the seventh birth-day or eighth year from conception young boys were handed over to the teacher of Arts whereas the Brahmin boys join the Vedic school after the initiation ceremony. They may however postpone the *upanayana* ceremony upto the sixteenth year from conception and in this case they shall have no choice other than joining the art-school. From birth to the child's first entry into school parents perform series of ceremonies. In this particular instance we may cite the example of Lord Goyama, a prince of the house of Bāravaī and the ceremonies performed by his parents from his birth to his first entry into art-school were as follows. "So the father and mother of little Goyama in due order performed the rites of the birth-day festival, the sight of moon and sun, the vigil, the name-giving, the walking and moving the legs, the feasting, the increase of food, the teaching to speak, the boring of the ears, the cleaning the ear, the dressing of the hair, the taking to school, and many other rites from conception to birth."[10]

Physical, emotional and mental growth are gradual ; and not sudden. There is a slow process of evolution. Like the modern psychologists the Jaina father recorded the tendency of the young boys to imitate adult occupations. It is a psychological fact with all the young boys and girls during the sekhā-stage which begins at the age of seven to dramatise adult occupations. Thus Hemacandra in his Sthavirāvalīcarita describes how Chandragupta, the founder of the Murya empire in his boyhood daily played the role of king with his co-villagers. He used to ride upon the boys when they played the role of elephants and horses. This is indicative of Chandragupta's

10. The Antagaḍadasāo And Aṇuttarovavāiya-dasāo, p. 23.

future fortunes.[11] The same view is stressed again in the Kathāsaritsāgara where the boys played the game of kingship.[12]

The gradual development of the physical, emotional and mental characteristics of the child upto the period of adolescence is a remarkable phenomenon to be noted and the Jaina authority Hemacandra noted this phenomenon with exactitude in the course of the child Goyama. We quote below an extract relavent to the point : "Their cheeks were like golden mirrors, and their eyes tender and soft like ears with beautiful wholes looked like pearl-oysters, and their necks purified by three lines, like conches. Their shoulders were arched like the frontal boss of an elephant, and their arms were long and fleshly like the king of serpents. Their breasts resembled slaps of Svarṇaśaila, and their navels were very deep like the mind. Their waists were slender as the middle part of a thunderbolt ; their thighs, straight and soft, had the shape of an elephant's trunk. Their legs were like the legs of a deer ; and their feet had straight toes like the petals of the sthalapadma."[13] With the physical changes in the adolescent youths of both sexes there is a change in their voice as well. "Further, satatasamitābhiyukta, the young man of good family or the young lady who keeps, teaches, proclaims, writes this Dharmaparyāya shall have an organ of taste possessed of twelve hundred good faculties of the tongue. ......A sweet, tender, agreeable, deep voice goes out from him, an amiable voice which goes to the heart, at which those creatures will be ravished and charmed ; and those to whom he preaches, after having heard his sweet voice, so tender and melodious, will even (if they are) gods, be of opinion that they ought to go and see, venerate, and serve him."[14]

Adolescence is marked by physical as well as by mental vigour. According to Jaina fathers intelligence begins to grow mature even from boyhood. "And this, after having passed childhood, and with just ripened intellect, having reached the state of youth, will become a brave, a gallant, and valorous king, the lord of the realm, with a

11. Hemacandra, Sthavirāvalī Carita, edited by Hermann Jacobi, p. 236.
12. Kathāsaritsāgara, vol. i, tr. by C. H. Tawney, M.A., p. 57.
13. Triṣaṣṭiśalākā-puruṣa-Caritra, vol. I, p. 72.
14. The Saddharma-Puṇḍarīka, tr. by H. Kern, pp. 346-347.

large and extensive array and train of waggons.[15] The modern psychological principle of individual differences was known to the Jaina fathers. One authority observes "Some men differing in intellect, will, character, opinions, taste, undertakings, and plans study various evil sciences." This is a fact which is borne by individual opinion. According to Kundakunda Ācārya high native abilities or talents are of four kinds : "Intuitive—'Autpattiki', Disciplined—'Vainayiki', the talent acquired by practice —'Karmaja' and developed talent or the talent acquired by the maturity of age, 'Pariṇāmiki."[17] This is a golden observation on which volume might be written : here is a plain truth borne out by experience. A Vālmīki or a Kālidāsa, or a Hemacandra is born with a poetic intution. No amount of study however vast, no discipline, however rigorous, no training however sedulous can make a Kālidāsa or a Shakespeare. But practice can develop the latent gifts of nature. By training the power of thinking, speaking may be developed. Automatic or habitual actions like speaking, walking, and moving and extraordinary feats like the gymnastic feats performed by professional athlets all belong to this category. The fourth type of talent is equally common. It is refreshing to read so much of sound common sense applied to the realm of psychology in our Jaina authorities.

The adolescent youths—males and females are fond of gangspirit and violence. They constantly move about in gangs. We already referred to such a story in connection with our lecture on female education. They are also fond of games, music and wild demeanour.[18] During this period young man or woman becomes social in their dealings with the public which earns him or her universal admiration. "That magnanimous young one......becomes a pleasure to the eyes of the people like the fullmoon."[19] This is followed by a period of adolescence : the period par excellence of Romance. "He, then, attained to youth which is a pleasure garden of Rati (or sport), a short weapon of cupid, and a charm to attract love-sick maidens."[20] We

15. Jaina Sutras, part, i, tr. by Hermann Jacobi, p. 240.
16. *Ibid,* p. 366.
17. The Nirayāvaliyāo, p. 16.
18. Rājaśekhara Sūri, Prabandhakoṣa, vol. i, p. 86.
19. Jaina Jātakas or Lord Ṛṣabha's Pūrvābhāsa, tr. by Amulya Charan Vidyabhushana, p. 28, verse no. 243.
20. *Ibid,* p. 28, verse no. 245.

quote again "The Master attained youth the opposite bank of the stream of childhood, majestic for the subjection of women."[21]

On the advent of adolescence, the manifestation of specific talent for music, dancing and singing becomes predominant. This is a principal fact biographically and psychologically borne out. There is a whole encyclopaedia of literature dealing with the topic.[22] Thus we see native and specific abilities and emotional traits—all grow concurrently with the physical growth of human organism. According to the Jaina as well as the modern psychologists the phenomenon of emotion is unsteady : it has flood and ebb-tides. "It is interrupted ; for oppositions are noticed in it, since we realize it as proceeding by the rise of good emotional karman disturbed by the rise of bad emotional karman.

"It is unequal, for it is utterly unsteady, since it evolves through increase and decrease. Thus even merit turns out to be, like sin, effective of pain."[23] Thus far our discussion of child and adolescent psychology has revealed the gradual growth of physical, mental and emotional traits of the growing child from birth to puberty. Now it will be our purpose here to trace how far and to what extent these psychological traits of the adolescent youths were taken into account in organizing the curricula of the art-school attended by the Princes or students of the ruling-class.

Curricula in the art-school were carefully organized with reference to the psychological factors referred to above. The whole range of the art-courses may be principally classified as follows : viz. (1) 3 R's, eg, reading, writing and arithmetic, (8) fine-arts : dancing, singing, music, painting and chivalry, (3) military-training with its allied sciences, (4) vernacular languages, (5) astronomy, astrology and other practical sciences. In course of time the Vedas and the Vedāṅgas were included in the curricula of the art-school. Of these the study of the 3 R's is of absolute necessity to give the children a command over the fundamental tools of knowledge. The fine arts were rightly included in the Jaina scheme of studies, as without them no liberal education

21. Triṣaṣṭiśalākā-puruṣa-Caritra, vol. ii, p. 318.

22. The Gaṇḍavyūha Sūtra, edited by Daisetz Teitara Suzaki And Hoki Idazumi, part. i & ii, p. 318.

23. Kundakundā Ācārya, Pravacanasāra, tr. by Barnard-Faddegon, p. 48.

was possible. Nothing is more calculated to develop the imagination and broaden the vision than poetry. Nothing can develop the visual perspective more effectively than painting. There is no severe indent to accuracy than sculpture. Nothing can aid the expression of the spirit more effectively than architecture ; and above all music is both an educator and medium of the true depths of the soul. To these purely academic branches of knowledge were added the supremely practical sciences of war. The following quotation will give us a faint idea of the state of things which then prevailed. "Now the royal prince, up to the time of his eighth year, grew up in the royal palace without any attention to study ; but from his eighth year till his twelfth year he was trained under the care of Viśvāmitra and Khāntadeva, as we have related.

"But now, having completed twelve years and being perfectly acquainted with all the customary modes of enjoyment, as men speak, such as hunting, riding and driving here and there, according to the desire of the eye or for the gratification of the mind, such being the case, it came to pass on an occasion that he was visiting the Kān-Ku-garden, and whilst there amused himself by wandering in different directions, shooting with his bow and arrow at directions, shooting with his bow and arrow at whatever he pleased ; and so he separated himself from the Śākya youths who were also in the several gardens enjoying themselves in the same way."[24]

The higher or the advanced courses in the Art-school such as vernacular languages, compositions, ballad-making, public-speaking, the Vedas, the Vedaṅgas, astronomy, astrology, the eight-branches of medicine, mineralogy and other sciences were pursued by the scholars for intellectual pleasure as well as for economic gain. Briefly speaking the whole range of the encyclopaedic courses in Arts were well adjusted to the physical, mental and emotional needs of the scholars from their boyhood to early adolescence and the whole syllabus was classified into four distinct groups, viz. 3 R's, Fine Arts, military-training, academic and scientific courses well organized on the sound basis of child and adolescent psychology beginning with the rudimentary subjects to the gradually increasingly difficult courses. Besides, the curricula of the

24. The Romantic Legend of Sākya Buddha, p. 72.

art-school were based on the realities of life taking into account the needs of institutions of society, viz. the family, the church, the state, the school and industry. Hence the curricula were vitally related to the realities of life. Specialization was the general rule, though the scholars were made to have an all-round training in all the courses.

The family, the school, the church and the state played a conspicuous part in the education of rulers of the States to fit them for their royal duties in time of peace and of war. It will be our purposes here to discuss the educational activities of each of these institutions of society.

In the Jaina literature we find evidences as to the educational functions of the family : it functioned not only biologically but also educationally. It helped the individual not only in the growth of his body but also in the development of his soul. The home was not only a castle but also a source of culture. The father was also the teacher. Thus Ṛṣabha taught his son Bharaha (Bharata) born to him by his wife, Yasavai the various arts, politics, sociology—embracing the social structure and machinery based on hereditary caste system and the civic duties of the members of the respective castes. He was also taught the geography of different Indian States, their inter-state relationships,[25]—and this is only a typical example.

School :—The Art and the Vedic schools existed in all the great cities and metropolis of ancient India such as Campaka, Rājagṛha, Vaiśālī, Kośala, Kapilavastu, and Bāravaī, Moḍerapuru and Pātalapura in Guzerat. Many such institutions of learning existed in the south and in other parts of India imparting useful and higher learning to the multitudes in India. Let us describe here some of the important art-schools wherein some of the leading princes received their all round education in these institutions of learning.

Education in the Art-school began at the age of eight from conception or seven years from birth which lasted till the dawn of puberty or adolescence. According to modern psychologists puberty for males begins at the age of fourteen and for the females at the age of twelve and childhood ends for both at the age of six. Eight-year curricula

---

25. Puṣpadanta, The Mahāpurāṇa, edited by Dr. P. L. Vaidya, chap. v, also p. 604.

for the males were instituted in the Art-school. "And when he passes from the state of childhood to that of youth, he will be perfect in all the common branches of knowledge."[26] But we learn from the "Lalitavistara" that Lord Buddha remained unschooled at the age of eight from conception or seven years from birth when he joined the writing or Art-school where he pursued the art-curricula up to his adolescence.[27] According to this source Lord Buddha studied in the art-school for seven years whereas according to the Jaina source the Art-school offered an eight-year course superimposed upon the pre-school or "infancy" school course where the children spent their days in organized games, and music along with other activities quite appropriate to their age. Thus prince Goyama of Bāravaī was sent by his parents to an art-school in an auspicious day at the age of eight from conception. "Then when his father and mother saw that little Gayama was past eight years of age, during an auspicious tithi, karaṇa day, star, and hour they brought him to a teacher of the Arts."[28]

The Art-school at Rājagṛha was also a popular institution offering academic, military, scientific and practical courses where pupils of all ranks went for education. Prince Mehā or Maghā, son of Śreṇika Bimbisāra was its student where he mastered the seventy-two Arts from his seventh year (eighth year from conception) till the dawn of his adolescence. "Then when prince Mehā was in his eighth year, his parents brought him to a teacher of the arts on an auspicious tithi, karaṇa and hour. The teacher of arts trained Mehā and taught him the seventy-two arts."[29] This wonderful curricula gives us an idea of the range, depth, and breadth of the Indian mind devoted to the solution of the problem of education. Here nothing is omitted, nothing is neglected. The education is as thorough and comprehensive as could be. Here again there is an encyclopaedic and ambitious scheme of studies demanding a knowledge of the seventy-two arts. A very high altitude of knowledge was reached and high degree of per-

---

26. The Kalpasūtra And Nava Tatva, tr. by Rev. J. Stevenson, p. 55.
27a. Lalitaviṣtāra, pp. 184, 190.
27b. Jātaka Stories, vol. I, tr. by Chalmers, p. 275.
28. The Antagaḍadasāo And Aṇuttarovavāiya-dasāo, p. 30.
29. Ardha-Māgadhī Reader, edited by Banarasi Das Jain, M.A., p. 101,

fection aimed at by those who were responsible for moulding the cultural destiny of India in that golden age of Indian culture and civilization.

In Kuṇḍinapura, a suburb of Vaiśāli, Vedic or higher institution of learning was superimposed upon the Art-school. This we learn from the dream which the mother of Lord Mahāvīra saw. In this post-graduate institution of learning the curricula included the Vedas, the Vedāṅgas, history, legends, philosophy, mathematics, grammar, prosody, astronomy and sacred texts of the Brahmins. "On leaving the state of childhood, he will be perfect in all the inferior branches of knowledge, and after entering on the state of youth, he will soon become able to repeat, defend, and uphold the four Vedas, the Ṛig-Veda, Yajur-Veda, Sāma-Veda, and the Atharva-Veda, and the Itihāsa (legendary history), which is considered a fifth Veda, and the Nighanṭu (lexicon), which may be termed a sixth ; the body divinity with all its members, know also their hidden meaning. He will be acquainted with the six subsidiary members of the Veda, and the sixth philosophical system (the Sāṅkhya), with the mathematics, the institute which directs its rites and ceremonies, grammar, prosody, analysis of words, astronomy, and other Brahmanical scriptures espicially that relating to the state of an ascetic ; in all of these he will become a proficient."[30]

Oudh :—Dr. Hemacandra gives us a vivid idea of the curricula of studies pursued by the ideal prince Sagara. This is slightly different from the curricula followed by the princes Goyama and Meghā. All the same it is very vast, comprehensive and almost oceanic. The following extract will give us an idea of the vast range of knowledge pursued by the ideal prince. "On the other hand, at the king's command, Sagara began to go to a teacher on an auspicious day, which was celebrated by a festival. In a few days Sagara absorbed the sciences, grammar, etc., like the ocean, the waters of rivers. Without effort Saumitri (Sagara) took the wealth of rhetoric from the teacher, like a torch taking light from another torch. He made his own sleep accomplish its purpose by poems, praises of passionless saints, flowers on the creepers of rhetoric, elixir for the ear. An ocean of learning and intelligence, he grasped unhesitatingly all the works of sacred authority, like deposits made by himself.

30. The Kalpasūtra And Nava Tattva, p. 27.

"Sagara defeated his opponents by unerring questions from the doctrine of Syādvāda, like Jitaśatru his enemies by arrows. He plunged into the unfathomable ocean of political science which had evil sea-monasters, filled with waves of the application of the six policies, of the (four) means, of regal power, etc. He learnt without difficulty the eightfold Āyurveda also, the torch of knowledge of the strength and effects of all herbs and essences. He acquired the science which is the source of knowledge about concerts, consisting of four kinds of musical instruments, four dramatic styles, and four modes of conveying pleasure. Without instruction he knew the characteristics of elephants complete with bites, states of mada, bodily characteristics, and medical treatment. He established in his heart by study and experience practices about draft animals and the characteristics of his horses and their treatment.

"He put his heart on archery and the characteristics of other weapons just from having them as easily as his own name. He attained skill in fighting with the bow, sword and shield, dagger, arrow, axe, lance, javelin, club, kampana, staff, spear, pike, plow-share, mace, cudgel, pattisa, duṣphoṭa, bhūsandhi, sling, arrow, trident, dart, and other weapons in conformity with the manuals. He became filled with all the arts like the full-moon with digits."[31] This shows how the capacious mind of the prince was equal, or rather more than equal to the Herculean burden laid on it by his teacher.

Arhat Ṛṣabha, the ruler of Oudh himslef taught seventy-two arts to his people for their benefit and as elsewhere writing was taught first and last of all astrology and here we have special reference to sixty-four arts meant for the females in addition to traditional seventy-two arts. Here we have clear mention of adjusting the curricula of the art-school to the needs of the fair sex. We quote below Ṛṣabha's curricula as follows : "The Arhat Ṛiṣabha, the Kosalian, clever with the aspirations of clever man, of great beauty controlling (his senses), lucky, and modest........During his reign he taught, for the benefit of the people, the seventy-two sciences, of which writing is the first, arithmetic the most important, and the knowledge of omens the last, the sixty-four accomplishments of women, the hundred arts, and three

31. Triṣaṣṭiśalākā-puruṣa-Caritra, pp. 68-70.

accomplishments of men."[32] These curricula in the Art-school at Oudh clearly prove it to be a co-educational institution admitting students of all ranks--males and females alike and the curricula were adjusted to their needs.

Art-school at Bāravaī :—

Prince Goyama of Bāravaī was sent by his parents to the local Art-school in an auspicious day at the age of seven. The teacher taught him the seventy-two arts. We quote below in support of our statement. : "The teacher trained little Goyama and taught him the seventy-two arts : firstly writing, then arithmetic as most important, and lastly bird's cries, in their text, purport, and practice—to wit, writing, arithmetic, inpersonation, dancing, singing, making music with instruments, with the voice, with the drum, and with cymbals ; gambling, popular conversation, dicing, play of the eight-square board, city-police, mixing of water with clay, rules of food, rules of drink, rules of house-keeping, rules of bed ; Āryā-verses, riddling, Māgadhī and Gāthā composition, ballad-making, śloka-making ; means of preparing unwrought and wrought gold, perfumes, and powders ; rules of ornament, attairing of damsels, points of women, of men, of horses, of elephants, of kine, of cocks, of umbrellas, of staves, of swords, of jems, and of the Kājani jewels ; lore of building, measurement of camps and cities, column and counter-column, flying column and fiying-counter, column, wheel-column, kite column, cart-column, fighting and heavy fighting, and supreme fighting, fist-fighting, arm fighting, branch-fighting, arrow-shooting, wielding the sword, lore of the bow, casting of unwrought and wrought gold, play with cells, with threads, and with lotus-stalks, engraving leaves, engraving bracelets, giving and taking life, and bird's cries. Then when he had trained little Goyama—the teacher of arts brought him to his father and mother."[33] The Jaina scheme of education in the art-school took note not only of the factors of pure knowledge and utility, but also of the factors of recreation which is so much needed for the proper development of the mind.

We can have an idea of the ways in which the Jaina monasteries

32. Jaina Sūtras, vol. ii, p. 282.

33. The Antagaḍadasāo And Aṇuttaravavāiya-dasāo, pp. 30-31.

discharged their educational functions from the accounts given below. Those monasteries educated the royal students with a view to their, competence for discharging the duties of the State ; and converted people including kings with a view to the exalted mission of the church. Thus the curricula of the Jaina monastery were admirably fitted to suit the needs of diverse duties of its alumni. The Jaina monasteries at the suburb of Bāravaī, Vārāṇasī or Benares converted prince Aimutte,[34] king Kanhe Vasudeva of Bāravaī,[35] and king Ālakkhe of Benares and king Ādayane[36] who pursued the eleven Aṅgas of the Jainas. They were not the only members of the royal-household to join the Jaina Order. King Ṛṣabha and his son Bāraha,[37] Mahāvīra Vardhamāna were all members of the powerful royal household who renounced the world for spiritual career.[38]

Art-school at Moḍerapura :—

Rājaśekhara Sūri, a much later authority describes a still different curricula for the education of the prince Āma, son of Yośavarman, king of Kanouj and his consort Sujasā. There lived a Sūri Siddhasena by name at Pātalipura in Guzerat during the reign of Jitaśatru. The Sūri repaired to the monastery at Moḍerapura where he trained Bappa Bhaṭṭi, son of Bappa, a Kṣatriya resident of Dūmbādhi in Pānchāla along with prince Āma of Konauj in the seventy-two arts[39] embracing the 3R's, fine-arts, military sciences, Vedas, Vedāṅgas, mineralogy, astronomy, astrology, medicine, treatment of plant-disease, and training of the Ācāryas etc. The curricula in Jaina monasteries were flexbile and varied. Thus Siddhasena Sūri's ideal curricula for the education of Bappa Bhaṭṭi and the prince of Kanouj are as follows :—

1 **लिखितम्** writing, 2 **गणितम्** arithmetic, 3 **गीतम्** singing 4 **नृत्यम्** dancing, 5 **पठितम्** reading, 6 **वाद्यम्** music, 7 **व्याकरणम्** grammar, 8 **छन्दो** prosody, 9 **ज्योतिषम्** astronomy, 10 **शिक्षा** phonetics, 11 **निरुक्तम्** etymology, 12 **कात्यायनम्** ritual, 13 **निघण्टुः** lexicography, 14 **पत्रच्छेद्यम्** cutting of leaves, 15 **नखच्छेद्यम्** cutting of nails,

34. The Antagaḍadasão And Aṇuttaravavāiya-dasão, pp. 84-85.

35. *Ibid,* p. 96. 36. *Ibid,* Loc. Cit.

37. Puṣpadanta, Mahāpurāṇa, vol. i, edited by P. L. Vaidya, p.

38. Jaina Sūtras, part I.

39. Rājaśekhara Sūri, Prabandhakoṣa, vol. „ p. 27.

16 रत्नपरीक्षा testing of jems, 17 आयुधाभ्यासः use of weapons, 18 गजारोहणम् riding elephant, 19 तुरगारोहणम् riding horses, 20 तयोः शिक्षा learning the use of arrows, 21 मन्त्रवादः science of mantra, 22 यन्त्रवादः science of surgical instrument, 23 रसवादः alchemy, 24 खन्यवादः mining, 25 रसायनम् chemistry, 26 विज्ञानम् science, 27 तर्कवादः logic, 28 सिद्धान्तः siddhanta, 29 विषवादः the science of curing poison, 30 गारुडम् the cure of snake bites, 31 शाकुनम् reading omens from the flight and cry of birds, 32 वैद्यकम् medicine, 33 आचार्यविद्या the science of teaching, 34 आगमः traditional doctrine, 35 प्रासादलक्षणम् architecture, 36 सामुद्रिकम् palmistry, 37 स्मृतिः law, 38 पुराणम् purāṇam, 39 इतिहासः anecdotes, 40 वेदः vedas, 41 विधि· injunction, 45 विद्यानुवादः interpretation of learning, 43 दर्शनसंस्कारः philosophy, 44 खेचरीकला yogic practice, 45 अमरीकला black arts, 46 इन्द्रजालम् magic, 47 पातालसिद्धिः an occult practice, 48 धूर्त-शम्बलम् cunning-art, 49 गन्धवादः perfumery, 50 वृक्षचिकित्सा treatment of plant-diseases, 51 कृत्रिममणिकर्म manufacture of artificial jems, 52 सर्वकरणी sundry art, 53 वश्यकर्म enchanting, 54 पणकर्म trade or business, 55 चित्रकर्म painting, 56 काष्ठघटनम् carpentry, 57 पाषाण-कर्म stone work, 58 लेपकर्म ointment, 59 चर्मकर्म leather work, 60 यन्त्रकरसवती manufacture of machines or implements, 61 काव्यम् poetry, 62 अलङ्कारः rhetoric, 63 हसितम् comic, 64 संस्कृतम् sanskrit, 65 प्राकृतम् prakrits, 66 पैशाचिकम् witchcraft, 67 अपभ्रंशम् apabhraṁśa prakrit, 68 कपटम् art of tricks, 69 देशभाषा spoken dialects, 70 धातु कर्म metal-work, 71 प्रयोगोपायः the mode of recitation, 72 केवलीविधिः the rule of the Kevalins.[40]

Having mastered this encyclopaedic curricula of a diverse nature the exiled prince of Kaunoj went to his father with his exiled mother who were warmly received into the palace by Yośavarman, the king

40. Rājaśekhara Sūri, Prabandhakoṣa, vol. i, p. 28.

and he nominated the educated young prince as his successor to the throne of Kaunoj.[41]

State :—State supervision over the education of the young prince was extended to Arts and higher education. The State encouraged specialization and specialists were sought for eagerly and they used to be appointed for the education of the princes. The Buddhist source supplies us with information on the point. Thus we learn from the legend of Śākya Buddha, that Lord Buddha, while a mere boy, received his education in the academic subjects and traditional sciences under Viśvāmitra in the regular class-room of the Art-school and his military training in Kān-Kui, the royal garden under Kṣāntadeva. The teacher were carefully selected in consultation with the wise ministers of the State. "Then the various ministers replied to the king as follows : 'Mahārāja, I know Viśvāmitra is most perfectly acquainted with all the Śāstras, and in every respect the most studied to become teacher of the prince, in all and every kind of scholar-like erudition. Then Śuddhodana despatched messengers to Viśvāmitra to speak to him thus 'Yill you, Oh, learned sir ! undertake to instruct the prince Royal in the various branches of polite learning and the usual manual accomplishments !'[42] We quote again "Then all the ministers respectfully answered the king and said, 'Mahārāja! the son of Supra Buddha, Kṣāntadeva by name, is thoroughly competent to teach the prince all the material accomplishments of which you speak'[43]" We learn also from the Jaina source that the military tactics were practised by the princes in a field especially set apart for this purpose called Khāturikā in the suburb of a capital city. The following extract will support our statemeant, "He wandered about until he arrived at the city of Sundaram where he happened upon Gunasundara, the son of the king of that city, practising military tactics on the field for military exercise (Khāturikā) outside the city."[44] Provision was also made for separate gardens or hippodrome for practising horse-riding as a part of military training for the princes or pupils of the art-school. Such "train-

41. *Ibid,* Loc. Cit.

42. The Romantic Legend of Sākya Buddha, p. 67.

43. Ibid, p. 70. ...... ..

44. Maurice Bloomfield, The Life and Stories of The Jaina Savior Pārśva nātha, p. 89.

ing-ground of horses was constructed in the suburb of Vasantapura, a city located at a distance of a month's journey from Kṣitipratiṣhthānapura and the next day after finishing the morning duties he went to the training-ground of horses at the proper time. He rode many horses from Balk, Turkey, and Vajjara, etc ; and sat in the garden of Sahasramaravana, situated on the skirt of the training-ground, for the purpose of removing its (i.e. of riding) fatigue."[45]

Military training was supplemented by physical training in its various aspects ; and for this extensive arrangement was made. The rulers systematically underwent physical exercises regularly each day for the preservation and development of their own health. Their physical exercises did not stop with the commencement exercises of their institutions of learning and it was prolonged during the rest of their lives. Hence like general education their physical education was also a continuous or life-long process. Thus according to Hindu or Jaina ideals physical well-being of human beings began in the pre-natal stage and lasted till the very end of human life. Consequently it is co-extensive with life. We have evidences of the physical exercises of the rulers and the public in the gymnasiums : the rulers underwent their physical exercises in their private gymnasium and the public in public gymnasiums of the city. Arrangements were also made for the constant supply of fresh-water for sanitary and hygienic reasons. Sometimes exercise-grounds were constructed on all sides of the swimming-pools as in Taxila. The rulers very early in the morning first underwent physical exercises with various instruments such as leaping, limb-twisting, wrestling, turning, stretching, arms with weights, practising the discuss and the javelin-throwing. Physical exercises were followed by ointment with oils scientifically prepared and diluted with drugs and perfumes. Experts in the science of ointment and rubbing, who were skilful, dexterous, accomplished, clever, wise, thoroughly conversant with the modes of rubbing, turning, used to rub the ruler with tender, delicate palms pleasant to the bone, flesh, skin, and hair with a view to comforting, inspiring, gladdening, strengthening, and rejoicing all the organs and limbs.[46] Gymnasium existed at

---

45. Haribhadra Sūri, Samarāicca-Kahā, (First Two Chapters) tr. by M. C. Modi, p. 19.

46. Jaina Sutra, part. ii, p. 420.

Taxila,[47] Kuśiṇagara,[48] Kuṇḍapura,[49] Bāravaī,[50] Avanti,[51] and at Nālandā.[52] The Licchavi youths practised military Arts in the gymnasium at Vaiśālī.[53]

Let us now turn to the description of a royal gymnasium at Kuṇḍapura, deriving our source-materials from the writings of various authors, devoted to the description of the aforesaid gymnasiums and thus to have a general view of a gymnasium in ancient India. We are quoting below to describe the royal gymnasium at Kuṇḍapura where king Siddhārtha, father of Lord Mahāvīra underwent his physical exercises. "Having got up, he went into the gymnasium, where there was a profussion of instruments for exercising the body, and weights for stretching the arms. There after exercising himself till he was tired and tired again, he took various kinds of oils some with a hundred and others with a thousand drugs and mendicants dissolved in them, sweet-smelling, nourishing, irradiating, exhilarating, flattening, strengthening, and quickening all the senses he anointed himself all over with these ; he was then well rubbed and shampoed by men skilled in the Art, and who could impart a softness and tenderness even to the palms of the hands and soles of the feet, who could perform their work with quickness and dexterity, fastness and cleverness of their profession, and who had studied well the Art, and were incapable of fatigue, kneading the body till the bones were invigorated, the muscles refreshed, the skin released, and hair made to shine, all the four tissues of the body refreshed and langour and fatigue banished. He then left the gymnasium, and went into the bathing-room."[54]

King Andhaga-Vaṇhi, lord of Bāravai had also according to the text similar physical training as comfortable as could be.[55] The above

---

47. The Indian Travels of Apollonius of Tyana and The Indian Embassies to Rome, tr. by Osmond De Beanrier Priaulx, p. 17.

48. Rajendra Lāl Mitra, Avadāna, p. 30, p. 73.

49. Jaina Sūtra, part I.

50. The Antagadadadasāo And Anuttarovavāiyadasāo, p. 20.

51. Vikrama's Adventure, p. 191.

52. The Jaina Sūtras, part. ii, p. 420.

53. The Kindred Sayings (Saṁyutta Nikāya), vol. iv, tr. by F. L. Woodward, p. 381.

54. The Kalpasūtra And Nava Tatva, pp. 57-58.

55. The Antagaḍadadasāo And Anuttarovavāiyadasāo, p. 20.

mentioned gymnasiums were well-planned and scientifically constructed and some of these were located in a huge garden with swimming-pools of cool-running water in the centre and had training-grounds for physical exercises on all rounds. "So saying, he led him to the place where he was accustomed to bathe. This was a garden-,—about a stadium long, with a swimming bath of cold running water in the middle of it on which side an exercising-ground."[56] Besides, some of these gymnasiums, again, had bathing-halls supported on innumerable pillars similar to the modern American gymnasiums. We quote below from the Jaina Sūtra to support our above statement. "This householder Lepa possessed, in a north-eastern direction from the suburb of Nālandā, a bathing-hall, called Seshadravya ; it contained many hundreds of pillars, and was beautiful."[57]

Thus our brief review of the education of the rulers or guardians of state reveals the truth that they pursued a comprehensive curricula embracing academic, technical, scientific, military and physical sciences so as to prepare them for State-service in time of peace and in war. The governing principle of the system of education pursued here was to maintain a complete equilibrium between the mind and the body. There was to be a perfect balance : a perfect harmony of the body and the soul. Here was a Platonic conception of education made more perfectly democratic and profound.

The State also controlled the education of the adult king. Adult-education was in vogue in ancient India and we have constant references to it in Jaina literature. The adult king received his education in the palace under a veteran teacher in the rudiments of learning as well as in advanced courses of studies, and politics under the general supervision of the minister. Night-class after the dinner used to be held for the education of the adult king with the permission of the minister. We have reference to such an education in the Prabandhacintāmaṇi where we get a fragmentary record of the education of Kumārapāla, king of Guzerat and a great patron of Hemacandra, the great Jaina leader. King Kumārapāla had a chequered career and had to fly for his life and pass the longer period of his life in disguise before he could

---

56. The Indian Travels of Apolonius of Tlana And The Indian Tmbassies, p. 17.

57. Jaina Sūtras, part. ii, p. 420.

establish himself as king of Gezerat. Consequently he could not receive education proper for a prince in his young days and had to engage a private-tutor to make up for the loss in the past. "Then, on another occasion, the king, named Kumārapāla, desiring to acquire learning, had the treatises of Kāmandaki on policy read to him for a time after dinner by a certain learned man, with the approbation of the minister Kapardin......after that speech, the king in order to comprehend the etymology of words, began the study of treatises, commencing with the alphabet, under a certain teacher, and in one year read three poems with their commentaries and so gained the title of Vicāracaturmukha."[58] The royal student mentioned here was not only a voracious reader but also a versatile genius.

Inspite of our limited sources of information, it seems to be pretty certain that classes in the Jaina Art-schools were held from sunrise to sunset, with a recess for the lunch ; and both group and individual instructions were in vogue. Group instructions were practised in case of training in military and cognate sciences, as it meant a good economy of time. Auto-education was encouraged in case of talented students like prince Siddhartha. The following quotation will bear us out on the point. "As for me" he said, 'I will be my own instructor :' on which Kṣānta-deva applied himself to perfect the five hundred young Śākya noblemen in all the Arts of his calling–riding the elephants, archery, chariot, racing and so on."[59] We learn from Hemacandra's Triṣaṣṭiśalākā-puruṣa-caritra, how Ajita Swamin, a teacher of military science was giving individual instruction to prince Sagara of Vinitā (Oudh).[60] The Poet Kālidāsa also favoured individual instruction for students of fine-Arts such as dancing, music and singing : and we learn from his Mālavikāgnimitram how Ganadāsa, teacher of fine-Arts taught Mālavikā the Art of dancing, music and singing in his own residence.[61] Similar method must have been in vogue in the other courses of the Art-school though we do not have definite proof of it.

In the Brahmanic school also individual as well as group instruc-

---

58. Merutuṅga Ācārya, Prabandhacintāmaṇi, pp. 138-139.
59. The Legend of Śākya Buddha, p. 70.
60. Triṣaṣṭiśalākā-puruṣa-Caritra, vol. II, p. 71.
61. Kālidāsa, Mālavikāgnimitram,

tion was followed. Thus, a teacher Soma by name expounded the śāstras to his son while he taught a group of students elsewhere in the school. "In due time, Soma had a son born to him, and, when he grew up, the father himself instructed him. While teaching a group of pupils he placed him in an underground chamber, sitting the while on a bench over it expounding the Śāstras."[62]

The materials at our disposal do not enable us to have an exact knowledge of the time-table followed in the Jaina school. There is reason to believe that physical and military exercises were held in the morning. Class-room instructions were given at noon. One course of instructions was followed by another, only after the first was completely mastered. Thus there was a distinctly scientfic method of learning. The following quotation gives us an idea of the method pursued. "That magnanimous young one, as he learnt up all the arts one after another, became a pleasure to the eyes of the people like the full-moon."[63]

But the Buddhists and the Hindu sources tell us a different story as to the programme of studies in the Art-school. We have noticed before in the lecture how Śuddhadhana, in consultation with his ministers, selected simultaneously Viśvāmitra and Kṣāntadeva to teach young Gotama the academic, art and military courses. The simultaneous appointment of the experts distinctly proves that the instructions in different branches of learning were concurrently given. All the aspects of the mind were to be simultaneously and thoroughly cultivated and trained. Complete education could ill afford to omit anything that contributed to culture of an ideal type. The point is not definitely stated in the "Legend of Śākya Buddha". It is our inference from the simultaneous appointment of the two teachers specialized in different branches of knowledge. But the Kathāsarit-Sāgara is much more definite regarding the simultaneous pursuance of the academic, scientific and military sciences at the same time. Thus Mahīpāla, son of Candra-Svāmin, a Brahmin learnt at the same time all the arts—academic, scientific and military. "And in course of time Mahīpāla grew up,

62. Maurice Bloomfield, The Life And Stories of The Jaina Savior Pārśvanātha, p. 84.

63. Jaina Jātaka, p. 28, verse no. 243.

and was taught the sciences of missle and hand to hand weapons, and was at the same time instructed in all knowledge."[64]

The method of teaching in the Art-schools and the higher institutions of learning was based on a sound educational psychology; and instruction whether in academic, scientific and in military subjects or in Vedic learning was never forced upon an unwilling mind. Education was adjusted to the natural bent of mind. This is true of music, singing, dancing[65] military sciences and in other academic subjects. Before admission to the military course, the prospective students had to demonstrate their fitness before the teachers by exhibiting their bodily strength, agility of motion and other attendant qualities. This is exactly what candidates for posts in the Army have to do all over the civilized world. Here we see the modern American practice of giving machanical aptitude test or try-out courses in technical, commercial or in any practical courses to discover the dormant abilities of pupils as a preparatory to their vocational and educational selection. We quote below to support our claim "He exhibited to the Lord the shooting a doll on a wheel, shooting an invisible object by sound, the shooting at a target in water, the shooting a clay-ball on a wheel with arrows. He showed pādagati, carrying a sword and shield,........He whirled rapidly a lance, spear, and club, giving the appearance of a fiery streak of lightning, revolving in the sky. He showed him knife-science with all the knife-positions, expert in all steps, like a dancer showing a dance. From devotion to his teacher and a desire to be taught by him he showed Ajita Svāmin his skill in other weapons also. Whatever was lacking in Sagara's arts—the Master taught him. For such a man has such a teacher. So both, engaged in activities according to their natures crossed the first period of life, like travellers crossing the boundary of a village."[66]

We have already discussed the method of teaching in connection with our lecture on "Monastic Education" which holds good in the case of education for the princes embracing academic, scientific and in

---

64. The Kathāsarit Sāgara, vol. ii, p. 549.

65. Kālidāsa's Mālavikāgnimitram, I, verse 14. also D. C. Das Gupta, Educational Ideas in Kālidāsa's India, Prabuddha Bharat, March, 1942.

66. Hemacandra : Triṣaṣṭiśalākā-puruṣa-Caritra, vol. II, p. 71.

military courses. We have already shown from the Jaina and the Buddhist sources how the blind-memory work was discarded in the ancient Indian educational system.

Nāgārjuna, the famous Buddhist scholar and preacher also bitterly assailed the blind-memory work in a vehement manner.

"Knowledge contained in books
And wealth procured from others,
When the time for needing them arrives,
Are neither knowledge nor wealth."[67]

And again "The superior man who has learned from books (only)
And has not studied (things) from many standpoints,
Resembles a pregnant girl of loose morals
He does not look well in an assemblage."[68]

Bitter criticism of blindly memorising the text does not dispense with the academic work altogether. The critics really mean that the pupils should thoroughly try to understand the piece or class assignment and then try to memorize it by "repetition." Of the five-fold process of studying[69] mentioned in the Jaina Sūtra, questioning the teacher, repetition, and pondering—these three steps in the process of studying are of great importance in learning any subject—academic, technical, scientific and military arts. Imitation in learning fine arts, military sciences or practical arts is of great importance. Kālidāsa was conscious of it and he advocated its utility in his Mālāvikāgnimitram where the heroine of the drama was learning fine arts in the house of Ganadāsa, her teacher by imitating him. "Imitation" is also mentioned in the Nyāya Sūtra of Gautama as an indispensable means of learning fine-arts. "When the pupil is taught, he only imitates what he finds in the teacher, as in the case with the teaching of dancing."[70] Imitation also played a prominent role in depicting through concrete illustrations the emotions and feelings of heart in painting. that is "imitation" is essential in painting. "The prince said it is proper for friends to imitate in words the conditïon of friends having first seen

---

67. *Ibid*, p. 84, verse 164.
68. *Ibid*, p. 118, verse no. 234.
69. Jaina Sūtras, vol, ii, p. 179.
70. Gautama, The Nyāya-Sūtra, tr. by Gaṅgā nātha Jhā, vol. ii, p. 83.

the painting. He asked for a pair of scissor to cut leaves. He carved in a betel-leaf the stately swan, in the same condition as that of a lady-swan, and strophe in clear terms to convey the heart."[71]

The ancient Jaina authorities rightly realised the importance of travels or tours as indispensable agents in the development of the mind. They were to supplement practically the theoretical training given in the schools. We have evidences of the practice both in the Jaina and the Jātaka literatures.

"King Ratnaśikha thus reflected. 'Without travelling to a foreign land one does not obtain glory, fame, knowledge of accomplishments, or anything. So I will certainly go to a foreign land and make trial of my merit........'Then the king formed a secret plan, and at the end of night he left the city, with his sword for his only companion, and went towards the north. Then, beholding many marvels in villages, assemblies, towns, and cities, relying everywhere on the power of his own merit, the king at last entered a terrible wood."[72]

Though scholars in the art-schools used to reside in the house of the teacher, such residence was not universal at a subsequent date. Scholars of such schools used to attend the classes from outside. We have clear evidence of it in the "The Life And Stories of the Jaina Savior." We learn from this source that one Kṣīrakadamba, a teacher had in his school prince Vasu, son of Abhicandra, king of Śuktimati along with his son Parvata and another boy named Nārada. At night they all studied on the roof of the palace.[73]

But we learn from the Kathākoṣa that Kṣīrakadamba was the teacher of a school in the city of Campaka. This establishes beyond doubt that Kṣīrakadamba's school was not a palace-school, it was a Brahmanic school. "In this very land of Bharata, in the village of Kuśasthala, dwelt a Brāhmaṇa, named Vasudeva ; his father died while he was a child....There he studied with a teacher named Kṣīrakadamba. He acquired fame among men as a student, and received alms in the king's palace."[74] Thus our brief survey of the education of the rulers

---

71. Haribhadra Sūri, Samarāicca-Kahā (First Two Chapters.) p. 81.

72. The Kathākoṣa, p. 140.

73. Maurice Bloomfield, The Life And Stories of the Jaina Savior Parśvanātha, p. 56.

74. The Kathākoṣa, p. 18

based on the fragmentary evidences in the Jaina literature, establishes the fact that the Indian princes of yore received their primary education in the popular schools along with children of the common people, where they used to master the whole range of encyclopaedic curricula, with a specialization in one particular branch of studies, according to their natural bent of mind. Physical and military courses occupied a prominent place in the programme of their education. They continued their education further in the Brahmanic school where they specialized in the Vedas, and the Vedāṅgas, and other varied courses. During the Jaina period, in the sixth century B.C. the Vedic school was superimposed upon the Art-school. Education was equally valued by the community at large as well as by the governing class. Ample provision was made for the liberal education of the princes to which the school, the church and the state contributed equally. Thus out of five social institutions, the above four except industry functioned as educational institutions for the education of the princes. The benefit of liberal culture was so much appreciated that even kings who, for good reasons, could have it in proper time would make up for the loss by appointing experts as private tutors for special training. The method of training followed was thoroughly scientific one. Thus we get here a very inspiring picture of the educational ideal followed by the rulers of India in the spacious days of the Jaina ascendency.

# LECTURE VIII

## VOCATIONAL EDUCATION

It is proposed to discuss in this lecture the vocations pursued in Jaina India with reference to their geographical origin, their geographical distribution, the application of psychological principles to vocational selection, and the organization and administration of vocations. The materials of this study, which represents a novel attempt of this kind, at any rate in this country, are derived principally from the Jaina sources supplemented by the Hindu and the Buddhist ones.

The geographical factors, viz. location, mountains, reliefs, bodies of water—inland or oceanic, soil, climate, flora, fauna, minerals, and the transportation systems have always,[1] in all ages and under all circuhstances exerted a paramount influence on the genesis, development, and the direction of the vocations of man, who, after all is a product of the environment, to a great extent. It has been so all over the world, and India is not an exception to the rule. Very naturally, we find all these factors powerfully effective in Jaina India. Let us now turn to the description of these factors, tracing their influence on vocations leaving out "location" for discussion in connection with the geographical distribution of vocations.

Mountain occupation :—

The mountain occupation is styled variously by different Jaina writers. Rājaśekhara Sūri names it vanajavṛtti (**वनजवृत्ति**) and Hemacandra styles it vanajīvikā (**वनजीविका**)[2]. According to the commentary of the Yogaśāstra, Vanajīvikā includes selling of fruits, flowers, leaves of wild-trees, either plucked or unplucked and the grinding of seeds with hand-mill.[3]

" **छिन्नाछिन्नवनपत्रप्रसूनफलविक्रयः ।**

**कणानां दलनात् पेषाद्‌ वृत्तिश्च वनजीविका ॥ १०२ ॥**

---

1. Huntington And Cushing, Principles of Human Geography, Chap. I.
2a. Rājaśekhara Sūri, Prabandhakoṣa, vol. I, p. 27.
2b. Hemacandra : Yogaśastra, vol. I, p. 566, verse 10
3. *Ibid*, pp. 567-568.

छिन्नस्य द्विधाकृतस्य अछिन्नस्य च वनस्य वनस्पति समूहस्य पत्राणां प्रसूनानां फलानां च छिन्नाच्छिन्नानां विक्रयो वनजीविकेत्युत्तरेण सम्बन्धः। कणानां च घरट्टादिना दलनाद्-द्वैधीकरणात्, शिलाशिलापुत्रकादिना पेषात् चूर्णीकरणाद्या वृत्तिः सा वनजीविका" ।[4] In addition to the aforesaid mountain occupations, trade in ivory is also peculiar to hilly tracts. Such regions are full of wild elephents, yaks and other wild animals which are assets to the hilly people for traffic in ivory, chamaris, nails, bones and hides. These occupations are styled as traffic in task or ivory by Hemacandra in his Yogaśāstra.

The influence of the soil, the climate, and the inland bodies of water on vegetation, and the growth and development of the animal population is immensely striking. The richness of vegetation, and the density of population greatly depend upon the fertility of the soil, excellence of the climate, and the adequacy of the supply of water. A glance at the populous regions of the world, like Europe, China, and India, will convince anybody of the truth of the remark. All these parts of the earth are blessed with a fertile soil or with a temperate climate, or with plenty of water-supply, or with all the three together. Of the human occupations, agriculture and herding of cattle are greatly influenced by the factors of soil, climate and water. These, however, are to be supplemented by the factors of human energy in all cases and by all means. With this brief preliminary remark, let us now discuss the occupational activities of ancient India pertaining to flora and fauna as described in the Jaina literature. Thus wheat, sugar-cane, and rice[5] were the agricultural products of the land, and cattle-raising was the occupation generally followed by the humbler folk. Oxen, buffaloes and rams[6] were available in large number. Naturally, agriculture and cattle-raising influenced the vocations of man living in a geographical region with fertile soil, ideal climate and plenty of water-supply. Briefly speaking, flora and fauna influenced the occupations of man in such an environment.

4. Hemacandra : Yogaśāstra, vol. I, p. 569.
5. Antagaḍadasāo And Aṇuttarovavāiya-dasāo, tr. by L. D. Barnett, p. I.
6. *Ibid*, Loc. Cit.

Fishery :—

Fishing industry is greatly influenced by water, climate, and soil. People living in the torrid zone, or on the sea coast, with a barren soil take to fishing occupation. This industry flourishes better in a cold climate than in tropical one with rich soil where people generally take to agricultural occupation. It is better and less costly to preserve the catches in the cold climate than in the tropical zone. Notwithstanding this disadvantage, people living in the tropical climate take to fishing occupation, on a moderate scale. Climate, soil and water also influence fishing industry in the warm climate. Here we are citing the case of fishing industry in ancient India carried on in the river Jumna : and the fishing industry in question was well organized with a chief as its head, who was assisted by hired labourers who were paid in cash. The following quotation supports our statement. "And at a certain time he became the head of the fishermen, who was irreligious (here the rest to be supplied SS 5-6 down to) difficult to be pleased. Then many men of that fisherman Soriyadatta, who were paid wages in cash or in food, used to plunge with boats (egaṭṭhiya) every morning into the great river Jumnā and used to capture many 'Saṇhamachhas'—kind of fish (here the rest to be supplied as above, down to) 'padāgas and aipadāgas' (kinds of fish), by means of draining off water from lakes –'dahagalaṇa', scrutinizing the lakes,–'dahamalaṇa', churning the lakes - 'dahamahaṇa,' destroying the lakes by removing water etc. —'dahavahana', draining off water from lakes—'dahapavahaṇa', various knids of nets for catching fish such as 'ayaṃpula' nets, 'panchapusla' nets, 'machaandhala' nets, 'machhapuchha' nets,—'jambhā' nets, 'tisirā' nets, 'bhisirā' nets, 'dhisarā' nets, 'visirā' nets, 'hillirī' nets, 'zilliri' nets, 'Jālas' angles to catch fish—'jālas', 'kūdāsa', nets, 'vakkabandhas'—kind of nets made of hemp, thread—nets 'suttabandhaṇa', and nets made of hair 'valabhandhana',–and used to fill the boats with those fish, take them to banks, make heaps of fish and expose them to sunshine . . . . . fried, baked and roasted, in the principal market of the city."[7]

Trade in Animals :—

The climate also determines the migration of birds and animals. Consequently the vocation of earning livelihood by the sale of birds is

7. The Vivagasuyam, tr. by V. J. Chokshi, & M. C. Modi, pp. 94-95.

conditioned by climate and soil. This vocation is called "असतीपोषणं" in the Jaina literature and it is looked upon with disfavour by the Jaina father. Such a vocation includes the rearing of sārikā, śuka, cat, dog, cock and peacock.

"सारिकाशुकमार्जारश्वकुर्कुटकलापिनाम् ।
पोषो दास्याश्च वित्तार्थमसतीपोषणं विदुः ॥"[8]

The occupation of boring lands includes the digging of wells, tanks, directing the river-course, draining the lakes, tilling agricultural fields, breaking stones, and manufacture of stone articles.[9] This occupation with its sub-groups is influenced by soil and the manufacture of stone articles are greatly determined by the soil and mountain reliefs. Wells or tanks cannot be dug in a soil which is likely to be silted soon. Nor agricultural occupation in a dry barren land can flourish. Traffic in lac"लाक्षावाणिज्य"[10] is also determined by soil, climate and mountains. Agricultural firms and floriculture in ancient India were well organized and workers such as guards were appointed by the ranchers to ward off birds and animals from the agricultural fields. The keepers of the field[11] and rice-fields are constantly mentioned in the Jaina literature.[12] Floriculture also flourished in rich fertile soil in an ideal climate and employees with various designations such as garden over-seers, keepers of the garden were attached to the gardens. In higher vocation such as medicine the influence of flora is also felt. The following quotation will support our statement. "Jivānanda learnt his hereditary science of Āyurveda in all its eight branches, and studied the drugs from the point of view of their taste, efficacy and action."[13]

As remarked in the foregoing pages, the soil and climate remarkably influence the growth of the animal population, which, again, determines human occupations such as agriculture, herding or grazing of

8. Hemacandra : Yogaśāstra, vol. I, p. 572, verse 113.
9. *Ibid*, p. 573, verse no. 114.
10. *Ibid*, p. 570, verse no. 108.
11. Kathākoṣa, p. 43.
12. *Ibid*, p. 45, p. 258.
13. Jaina Jātakas, p. 77, verse no. 729.

cattle,[14] elephant-driving,[15] the occupations of the butcher,[16] fisher-folk,[17] the snake-catchers,[18] the leather-workers, the ivory-workers etc.[19]

The soil also determines the transportation system. In the mountainous regions it is quite different from the one in the plains. In ancient India as in other parts of the country of the civilized world human and animal power was utilized in the transportation system. Even to-day human and animal agencies are in vogue in mountainous regions where modern transportation system cannot be introduced with profit. The Jaina literature mentions "शकटजीविका" and "भाटकजीविका" as two distinct types of occupations in connection with the transportation system. The former includes the manufacture of vehicles, their parts, and their sale together with the beasts of burden either personally or by agents. Earning livelihood by such occupation is called traffic in vehicle.[20] The rearing of oxen, buffaloes, camels, donkeys, mules and horses to be used in drawing vehicles is called "भाटकजीविका"[21]. Another distinct type of occupation was developed in ancient India in connection with the branding of animals known as "निर्लाञ्छनकर्म". This occupation is concerned with the branding of cows, buffaloes, horses and other domesticated animals., and their castration, branding the back of young elephants and boring the ears.[22]

The Minerals :—

Minerals were closely connected with the development of Indian civilisation in its commercial or purely material aspect. It was what one might naturally expect, in view of the immense natural resources

14. Kathākoṣa, p. 120, p. 78.
15a. *Ibid,* p. 141.
15b. Kathāsarit-sāgara, p. 83.
16. The Book of Discipline, vol. I, tr. by J. B. Horner, p. 113.
17. The Vivagasuyam, pp. 94-95.
17a. Kathākoṣa, p. 168.
18. Mudrā Rākṣasa, pp. 19, 23.
19a. Hemacandra : Yogaśāstra, vol. I, p. 566, verse no. 10.
19b. Amaracandra Sūri, Padmānanda Mahākāvya, p. 592, verse no. 425.
20. *Ibid,* p. 568, verse no. 104.
21. *Ibid,* verse no. 105.
22. *Ibid,* p. 572, verse no. 112.

of this land. Many European authorities think otherwise, but their opinions, without hesitation may be attributed to pure dogmatism begotten of ignorance. We give below a list of occupations connected with minerals as given by the Jaina authorities. These are the occupations of goldsmiths, jewellers,[23] chief-jewellers,[24] jewel-testers,[25] braziers (kosakara),[26] workers in metals including gold, silver[27] and copper.[28] Mineral-occupations are mentioned in the Yogaśāstra under the category of traffic in poison. The list includes swords, ploughs, deadly weapons and spades. The sale of these deadly weapons is called traffic in poison.[29] These mineral-occupations received fuller treatment in the Mahābhārata. Hemacandra, in the Yogaśāstra, vol. I, mentions vocations regarding machinery for pressing sesamum, oil-seed, pressing sugar-cane and water-mill.[30] It is hard for us to tell from Hemacandra's description of the machinery and from the commentary whether these implements were made entirely of wood or of iron. At any rate, these machines must have been made of both wood and iron. Vocations concerning the manufacture of charcoal are also influenced by mountains for they are dependent upon the supply of timber from forests. It is styled as Aṅgārajīvikā in the Jaina literature. The charcoal was utilized according to the commentary of the Yogaśāstra in frying cereals, in baking earthen pots, in preparing medicinal herbs, in smelting iron, silver and gold.[31] Traffic in lac[32] was also greatly influenced by mountains along with the soil and the climate. Soil, climate and water also determine greatly the higher needs of human life, viz. politics, religion, science and education. All these aspects of human civilization are the products of the three factors mentioned above. Limited space and time forbid the lengthy discussion of these aspects

---

23. Triṣaṣṭiśalākā-puruṣa-Caritra, vol. II, p. 191.
24. *Ibid,* p. 81.
25. Prabandhacintāmaṇi, p. 104.
26. Padmānanda Mahākāvya, p. 592, verse no. 8.
27a .*Ibid,* verse no. 2.
27b. Triṣaṣṭiśalākā-puruṣa-Caritra, vol. II, p. 191.
28. *Ibid,* Loc. Cit.
29. Hemacandra : Yogaśāstra, vol. I, p. 571, verse no. 101.
30. *Ibid,* verse no. 111.
31. *Ibid,* p. 567, verse no. 102.
32. *Ibid,* p. 570, verse no. 108.

of human occupations. Besides we have touched upon State vocations in connection with our lecture no. IV.

Having narrated the influence of geographical factors on vocations, let us now turn to the discussion of their geographical distributions. Here the influence of 'Location' is predominant.

(a) Campaka :

Let us now begin with Campaka. We have discussed the topography of Campaka in connection with our lecture no. V. Repetition has become here an unavoidable necessity for tracing the relationship between the topography of the city and her occupational activities. The city itself was covered with a net-work of roads; and in it there were plenty of vehicles such as chariots and palanquins, litters and carriages, all of which were used for the purpose of transportation. As might be expected in a centre of commerce, there were good many markets for the distribution of goods ; and there were places meant for the purpose of walk and excursions so essentially necessary for the preservation of health of the citizens. Favourable climate and excellent situation contributed to the density of the city's population all of whom were engaged in agricultural and cognate pursuits. Almost as a matter of course it developed into a brisk commercial centre resorted to by princes, aristocrats and other dignitaries.[33]

As a corollary to the commercial prosperity of Campaka, its architectural grandeur followed as a matter of course, affording room for activities to skilled artizans. One ancient authority testifies to the splendour of the city thus "Its bastions, rampart-paths, doorways, gates and arches were lofty, its high-roads duly divided. Its gate-bars and bolts were stout, and fashioned by skilful artificers. It contained markets and bazars thronged with craftsmen, content and happy."[34]

Development of fine arts other than architecture, notably music necessarily followed ; theatrical arts began to flourish and there were innumerable actors and actresses contributing to the gaity us well as to frivolity of the citizens. The following words of the text give us an idea of this ancient city in its higher aspects. "It was liberal in almsgiving, a home of secure and pleasant life, dense with many millions

---

33. The Antagaḍadasão And Aṇuttarovavāiya-dasão, p. I.
34. *Ibid,* Loc. Cit.

of citizens content and happy. It was haunted by actors, dancers, rope-walkers, wrestlers, boxers, reciters, jumpers, ballad singers, storey-tellers, pole dancers, picture-showmen, pipers, lute-players and clappers in plenty."[35]

(b) Rājagṛha :

Let us now come to the military city of Rājagṛha, the capital of Magadha. It was situated in the midst of five mountains and thus was impregnable against any possibility of foreign attacks. We can not know much about it from the Jaina source which is to be supplemented by the Buddhist text which tells us a good deal about it.

We learn from Buddhist sources that the citizens of Rājagṛha had recourse to hunting, and the training of animals and thus the not very dignified occupations of the fowler and the deer-hunter came into being, and the butchers were sub-divided and refined into cattle-butchers, sheep-butchers and pig-butchers. It is needless to say that the genesis and development of these occupations were influenced by the hilly environment of the city, the hills being the abodes of all types of animals and birds. The Lord Buddha himself resided in a region five hundred *li* from Rājagṛha where there lived a mountain clan of hunters consisting of 122 persons. Over and above, the occupation of cattle-raising flourished in the suburb of Rājagṛha. Curiously enough, the cattle-raisers were all Brahmins by birth. This occupation flourishes owing to the luxurious growth of grass due to the mountainous regions near by. Authoritative words may be quoted, "In days of old, at the back of the Gṛdhrakūta mountains, near Rājagṛha, there was a village, of some seventy or so families, all of them Brahmans. Buddha wishing to convert these people, came to the place and sat down under a tree.

....To this they replied—'we have dwelt here during thirty-generations past, and our occupation is to tend cattle."[36]

The climate of Rājagṛha was also favourable to the growth of floriculture ; and we are told of Ajjunae a rich florist of the city. This science required a thorough and systematic study and reached to a great perfection. We are told of the sage who came from the Sripar-

---

35. The Antagaḍadasāo And Aṇuttarovavāiya-dasāo, pp. 1—2.
36. Dhammapada, tr. by Samuel Beal, p. 64, verse no. 2.

vata to the royal court and taught the king the valuable science. Inland bodies of water too exerted remarkable influence on the activities of Rājagṛha who found it profitable to fish in the river, the Tapoda, the Ganges and the lakes adjacent to the city.

As might be expected, all the dignitaries of the State resided in the capital city. Very naturally, there was a governmental department exercising control over the forest which existed on and near the mountains adjacent to the city. We read actually of the premier of Magadha conducting business tour and coming into contact with the overseer of the wood apparently an officer of the forest department.

(c) Vaiśālī :

Besides agriculture, commerce, architecture and the arts relating to amusement flourished vigorously. State vocations flourished in the inland cities as a matter of course. There the form of Government was constitutional. Strong centralized government is possible only in rich fertile soil. We learn from the Kalpasūtra the existence of the State occupations at Vaiśālī to be as follows :—

(1) Vice-regent, (2) Cabinet-ministers, (3) Counsellors, (4) Heads of departments, (5) Commander of troops, (6) Commander of forces, (7) Commander of chariots, (8) Heads of police, (9) Chief of the royal messengers, (10) Warders, bankers, astrologers, sealers, and slaves. To this list we may add the following occupations of amusement in addition to the one we already described at Campaka such as players on cymbals, on tambouriners, wind and stringed instruments, and on those who toss up poles and double balls.[37]

(d) Bāravaī (Dvārakā) :

Let us now turn to the description of the influence of the environment upon the occupational activities of a coastal town namely the city of Bāravaī (Dvārakā) within the vicinity of the Arabian sea. We learn from an authoritative source that a good number of occupations flourished there connected with the activities of the State. There were kings and princes and barons ; and where there are these dignitaries, there are commerce and commercial activities. In consequence we find bankers, traders and merchants. We can get a glimpse of the various

37. The Kalpa-Sūtra And Nava Tattva, p. 77.

types of occupational activities that sprang up into being in connection with the court-life.

Thus there were stuffs, pikes and bows and so forth. There were persons with the lyres and caskets. There were wand-bearers, shavellings, jesters, jokers, and buffons. In other words the light as well as the grave aspect of life were thoroughly represented in this important city in the days of yore.[38] It goes without saying that the prosperity of the citizens with its various activities was possible only because of their commercial prosperity which again was greatly influenced by the favourable position of the city on the site of the sea.

(e) Polasāpura :

Polasāpura, an inland city illustrates significantly though not exactly, the influence of geographical factors on the material prosperity of the citizens. The city owed its greatness principally to commercial factors. Commerce was very brisk there and it was followed by prosperity. There were various types of industries actively carried out by the people of the city. Pottery was one of the industries which flourished vigorously in the suburb of the city. It received a scientific treatment and was noted for specialization. The principle of the divison of labour was in evidence. Some of the workers were engaged in bowels, others in pots and so forth. There were manufacturers as well as salesmen as in modern towns with this difference that the capitalistic manufacturers took advantage of their superior position by exploiting the workers.[39] Thus our brief review of the topography of the above mentioned cities gives us an idea of the occupational activities of the citizens as quite different from those living in the hilly regions where hunting, selling wild fruits and roots are the prevailing types of occupations.

At the initial stages of the Indian civilization, vocational and educational selections were greatly determined by the institution of caste with its spirit of narrowness, rigidity and seclusion. Then came the tremendous assaults on caste by Jainism and Buddhism with the result that the rigour of caste came to be modified. The change had its effects in the field of education. "Child-Life" came in consequence, to

38. The Antagaḍadasāo And Aṇuttarovavāiya-dasāo, pp. 21, 49, 51.
39. Uvāsagadasāo, p. 119.

be recognized as the standard of occupational and educational selection. In order to have an idea of the vocational selection made on the basis of caste we have to refer ourselves, to Manu and other authorities. Thus Manu advocates vocational selection on purely caste-system in the following verses. "A man of low-caste who through covetiousness lives by the occupations of a higher one, the king shall deprive him of his property and banish.

It is better (to discharge) one's own (appointed) duty incompletely than to perform completely that of another ; for he who lives according to the law of another (caste) is instantly excluded from his own."[40] Vaikhānasasmārtasūtram makes similar injunction in occupational and educational selection only to preserve the existing social order of the time.[41] The Mahābhārata recommends the three principal groups of vocations to be adjusted to the three principal classes of people viz. the highest, the middle and the lowest classes of people to avoid chaos in vocations, that is, to eliminate vocational mal-adjustment. Though in the Mahābhārata the element of caste system is advocated in vocational choice yet premium is placed upon efficiency and intelligence in vocational training and placement. Thus the following verse will support our claim.

"कश्चिन्मुख्या महत्स्वे मध्यमेषुच्च मध्यमाः ।
जघन्याश्च जघन्येषु भृत्याः कर्म्यासु योजिताः ॥"[42]

Rigidity of the caste-system was not strictly adhered to in vocational and educational selection during the Buddhist period and education was completely democratized. Scholars in collaboration with their parent or parents made a thorough selection of their life's calling so as to fit the profession into their natural bent of mind which would enable them to live as a self-respecting citizen in the State. The following quotation will support our contention. "When Jiwaka, who was also called Kumarabhacha, was seven or eight years of age, he was playing with the princes in the hall, and they reproached him with having no mother. Ashamed, he went to Abhaya, and asked who was his

40. Manu, p. 423, verse nos. 96, 97.
41. Vaikhānasa Smārtasūtram, tr. by D. W. Caland, p. 225, p. 231.
42. Mahābhāratām, p. 46, verse no. 43.

mother ; but he smiled and said, 'I am your father, who was your mother I do not know ; I found you exposed in the forest, and rescued you.' Then Jīwaka reflected, when he heard this circumstance related, that he would receive no inheritance from relationship ; so he resolved that he would learn some science, and then by his attainment he might be able to acquire both relatives and wealth.

Again he considered the character of the eighteen sciences and the sixty-four arts, and determined that he should study the art of medicine, that he might be called doctor, and be respected, and attain to eminence ; with this intention he went to Taksala, and applied to a learned professor to receive him into his school."[43] This is what might be expected of a man of real genius.

Imagination of the acutest and finest type was exercised by the parents of ancient India in the selection of the occupation of their children. This important affair was never left to chance but was guided by a rich imagination. This point is clear from the theory and practice of the Jaina and the Buddhist authorities who took into full account the factors of occupational environment, and the ability of the student. In a word financial profit, material comfort, future prospect, social status—all these entered into the minds of the Buddhist parents in the selection and rejection of the occupation of their wards. As a typical evidence we may insert a quotation from the Vinaya Text describing the scrupulous and judicious care exercised by the parents of Upāli in selecting the occupation of their son. "At that time there was in Rājagṛha a company of seventeen boys, friends of each other, young Upāli was the first among them. Now Upāli's father and mother thought: 'How will Upāli after our death live a life of ease and without pain ? Then Upāli's father and mother said to themselves ; if Upāli could learn writing, he would after our death live a life of ease and without pain.' But Upāli's father and mother thought again : If Upāli learns writing, his fingers will become sore. But if Upāli could learn arithmetic, he would after our death live a life of ease and without pain.'

But then Upāli's father and mother thought again : 'If Upāli learns arithmetic, his breast will become diseased.' But if Upāli could learn

43. Manual of Buddhism, tr. by Hardy Spence, pp. 238-239.

money-changing, he would after our death live a life of ease and comfort, and without pain.' But then Upāli's father and mother said to themselves : 'If Upāli learns money-changing, his eyes will become sore. Now here are the Śākyaputtiyā Samanas, who keep commodious precepts and live a commodious life : they have good meals and lie down on beds protected from the wind. If Upāli could be ordained with the Śākyaputtiyā Samanas, he would after our death live a life of ease and without pain.'[44]

It is startling and interesting to note that Jaina authorities advocated a system of vocational guidance on the basis of collaboration between the parents concerned and the general body of citizens at large. Here was a distinctly modern and a democratic touch. The city supervisors of morals used to call such conferences which assisted the youths in the careful selection of their occupation. Let us quote Haribhadra Sūri on the point. "Then the citizens were informed. They liked it very much. Their parents were called. The whole matter was narrated to them. They also liked it very much. Then they were made to make a promise. 'You should not put them to difficulty.' Dharana and Devanandi were then called. Each of them was given goods of the value of five lacs of Dinaras. The document was drawn up."[45] The point is much more explicitly and clearly stated in the Triṣaṣṭiśalākā-puruṣa-Caritra where prince Sagara made a demonstration of his skill in the various aspects of military science before Ajitaswamin out of his desire to be taught by him. The natural bent of mind was taken into account in teaching the military science. Sagara's demonstration before his teacher Ajitaswamin is similar to the modern practice of administering performance tests to students of vocational education in U.S.A. The following quotation will bear us out. "From devotion to his teacher and a desire to be taught by him he showed Ajita Svāmin his skill in other weapons also. Whatever was lacking in Sagara's arts the master taught him. For such a man has such a teacher. So both engaged in activities according to their natures..."[46] Intelligence as the basis of vocational success is also stressed in the Prabandhacintāmaṇi.

---

44. Vinaya Text, vol. I, pp. 201.
45. Haribhadra Sūri, Samarāicca Kahā, p. 10.
46. Triṣaṣṭiśalākā-puruṣa-Caritra, vol. II, p. 71.

We quote below to support our statement. "Being naturally clever, he had read such books as the Agastyamata, and the Ratnaparīkṣā of of Buddhabhatta, and from living in the company of jewel-tester he had become expert in the discrimination of jems."[47] Intelligence as the sound basis of professional success has also been stressed in the "Vivagasuyam" the eleventh Aṅga of the Jaina canon. It is said in the above canon that a good many medical practioners who had been to the house of Soriyadatta, the chief of fishermen, to extricate a fish-bone from his throat used their utmost skill by applying the 'Four Talents' only to meet a with total failure. We quote below to support our claim. "Then many physicians heard this proclamation while it was being announced, and having done so they went to the house of Soriyadatta and went to where the fisherman Soriyadatta was lying, and making use of their, 'Four Talents Viz. (1) Intuitive—'Anutapattiki', (2) Disciplined—'Vainayiki. (3) the talent acquired by practice 'Karmaja' and (4) Developed talent or the talent acquired by maturity of age 'Parinamiki', they tried to extract the fish-bone out of the neck of the fisherman Soriyadatta by means of vomitting, medicines to vomit, a pain-going treatment (such as beating, striking or rubbing hard the diseased part of the body)."[48] Reference to the application of 'Four Talents' by the medical practioners has again been made in the above cannon in connection with the vajinal treatment of the consort of king Vijaya.[49] This practice proves conclusively the firm conviction of the Jaina fathers, in the efficacy of the 'Four Talents' in professional success. "Business Talent" is also mentioned in Karakaṇḍa Cariu as a basis of professional success. "Who charmed the king by his business-ability,"[50] intelligence or specific talent as the basis of occupational or vocational selection has been much more clearly advocated in the writings of subsequent Hindu writers. We quote below to substantiate our statement. "When they heard this speech of the kings one of them said—'I am Pañchaphuttika by name, a sudra ; I possess a peculiar talent or I weave every day five pairs of garment."[51]

47. Kathākoṣa, p. 104.
48. The Vivagasuyam, p. 96.
49. *Ibid*, p. 144.
50. Muni Kanakāmara, Karakaṇḍa Cariu, tr. by Hirālal Jain, p. 190.
51. Kathāsarit Sāgara, vol. I, p. 449.

This evolution of the standard of vocational selection in ancient India was an interesting, slow and a tentative process. There was a transition from a dull, mechanical, aristocratic to a vital, rational and democratic criterion. The ideals of aristocracy came to be replaced by the ideals of personality—of personal competence. The germ of this democratic ideal may be traced to the Mahābhārata. It was developed in right earnest by the Buddhists and the Jainas. The Buddhists experienced the influence of the work on the workers—a vital thing. The Jainas wanted to make education a concern of the State in a spirit of racial democracy. The Hindu writers wanted to adjust the vocations to the talents of the votaries. Thus there was a constant progress in the direction of balance, harmony and perfection. Hence as in the modern period vocational guidance was practised in ancient India.

Let us now turn to the discussion of the final phase of vocational education in Jaina India. In imparting vocational education to the future citizens of the State, the Family, the Church, the School, the State, and Industry—the five great institutions, were always active. We have elsewhere dwelt on the important and effective parts played by them in moulding the educational system of India and thus moulding the very soul of Indian civilization and culture.

The State, centuries before the Christian era, when Jainism was in the ascendent took keen interest in the welfare of its citizens and for its furtherance introduced agriculture, trade, industry and diverse vocations so essential to supply the physical needs of human life. There is textual evidence to show that Lord Ṛṣabha was keenly interested in the promotion of vocational education of the people. Thus the Lord taught the citizens of his State five silpas, exhorted them to settle down into agricultural life and to various gainful occupations. We quote below to illustrate the five silpas.

"तक्ष-चित्रक कुविन्द-नापिता-नातनोदिति सपञ्च शिल्पिनः। ग्राम्यमी तु शतधाऽभवन यतो विंशतिप्रकृतिरेक पकफः"[52]

Hemacandra, the great Jaina leader of the Śvetāmbara sect stressed the same point when he ascribed to Lord Ṛṣabha of Vinita (Oudh) the introduction of vocations concerning food, clothing and shelter—the

52. Padmānanda Mahākāvya, p. 208,

three fundamental needs of human life. We quote below from Hemacandra relating to this point "From that time, the first artisans, the potters, arose. For the sake of houses for the people, the Lord appointed carpenters. He, wise, appointed painters for the painting of the houses, for the sake of diversity of the people's pleasure. He established weavers for the people's clothes ; . . . . . . . . .

The Master, the sole father of the world, appointed barbers for the people who were very much annoyed by the growth of hair and nails. . . . He established grass-gathering, wood-carrying, ploughing, and trade—these business for the sake of the people's livelihood."[53] Here we find the modern conception of the State patronage of agriculture, trade, commerce and industry for the financial prosperity of the citizens, clearly anticipated. This patronage was effectively supplemented by industrial training given to fit students.

In ancient India—in Jaina India—the employment of the citizens of the state after their period of training was over, was a concern of the government. This ultra-modern theory was thoroughly understood and practised by the Jaina authorities. The conference of parents and citizens at large to which we have already referred is an instance to the point. The Mahābhārata bears clear testimony to the consciousness of the rulers in this important aspect of their duty. The following quotation from the Mahābhārata will bear us out.

" द्रव्योपकरणं कच्चित् सर्व्वदा सर्व्वशिल्पिनाम् ।
चातुर्म्मास्यावरं सम्यङ् नियतं सम्प्रयच्छसि ॥ ११९ ॥
कच्चित् कृतं विजानिषे कर्त्तारञ्च प्रशंससि ।
सतां मध्ये महाराज ! सत्करोषि च पूजयन्[54] ॥ १२० ॥"

Cāṇakya in his famous Arthaśāstra advocates the state supervision of trade and industry ; and there he mentions a separate department of trade and industry with a hierarchy of officers.[55]

The ancient merchants, tradesmen, artizans, agriculturists and other businessmen had associations or guilds of their own. We have

---

53. Triṣaṣṭiśalākā-puruṣa-Caritra, vol. I, p. 152, p. 153.

54. Mahābhārata, vol, iv, p. 69, verse nos. 119-120.

55. Cāṇakya's Arthaśāstra, tr. by R. Shama Sastry, pp. 94, 100, 106, 140. 180-181.

no detailed information about such associations from the Jaina sources at our disposal. Hemacandra makes incidental reference to such a guild of washermen[56] in his Sthavirāvalīcaritra. In the Vivagasuyam, the eleventh Aṅga of the Jainas reference is made to a chief of fishermen—a chief of the guild of fishermen.[57] We learn, however, from Buddhist sources of such associations of merchants. Mention is made therein of five hundred merchants in India who had an association with Maitri as its president. The merchants freely took counsel from this association regarding their overseas-trade and ocean-navigation. The association of merchants had various departments over which supervisors were appointed by themselves. "I remember in years gone by,—there were 500 merchants in Jambudwipa, of whom a certain one was chief, his name being Maitri (sse—che). On one occasion, these merchants all assembled together, and began to consult how they might best embark on some expedition for the purpose of getting gain. ....Then the merchants having assembled on the coast, and offered their worship to the sea-god, selected five men to superintend the various departments (as before), and then set sail."[58]

We learn from Viṣṇu of the status of the Association, something about the Guilds of merchants, businessmen or artizans and other professional groups of autonomous bodies. Severe punishment used to be inflicted on those treacherous members of the Association who attempted to create dissension and chaos among its members by their unlawful act. The state intervention is sanctioned by Viṣṇu to punish those mal-creants for the preservation of the Association from ruin. "Those who cause dissension among the members of an association, shall undergo punishment of a especially severe kind; because they would prove extremely dangerous like an (epidemic) disease, if they were allowed to go free. Wherever a criminal act, opposed to the dictates of majority, has been attempted, a king desirous of prosperity shall redress it."[59] The president of the Guild according to this authority should spring from a noble family, should be versed in the Vedas,

56. Hemacandra : Sthavirāvalicaritra, p. 206.

57. Vivagasuyam, tr. by V. J. Chokshi, and M. C. Modi, p. 20.

58. The Romantic Legend of Śākya Buddha, pp. 342-343.

59. The Minor Law Books, p. 155, verse no. 6,

should be dutiful, energetic, bear good moral character and be skilled in different phases of industry.[60]

The Association or Guild of merchants should appoint counsellors to advise the villagers, companies of artizans and other associations.[61] In the Samarāicca Kahā, we have reference to a king's commission composed of five principal citizens, which accompanied Dharana and Suvadana to the sea-shore, and which counted gold and handed it over to the former. This passage suggests to us the practice of appointing an advisory board similar to the one advocated by Viṣṇu in his code.

We quote below a relevant extract. "Then being headed by the commission of principal citizens from the king, Dharana, along with Suvadana went to the shore. The gold was counted by the committee and was handed over to Dharana."[62] Thus the Hindu and the Buddhist literatures support the Jaina view of the state patronage of agriculture, industry and commerce and the placement of the future citizens. The State extended its co-operation to Associations or Guilds of merchants, businessmen, artizans and agriculturists and constantly helped the people in their profession either by appointing special commission or through the advisers of the association.

This authority describes rules and regulations which remind us of their counterparts in mediaeval Europe,—compulsory residence, fixed period of training, the spirit of rigid seclusion, and above all the phenomenon of corporal punishment for the deserter. The apprentice received free instruction, room and board and had to pay the honorarium voluntarily to the teacher at the time of his returning home. Thus vocational education was virtually free and compulsory.

The instruction in the house of the teacher and the work in the factory or farm were simultaneous. The teacher was very cautious to place his apprentice on the appropriate occupation for which he was receiving theoretical instruction in the school. Thus there was proper co-ordination between work in industry and teaching in the school. The income of the apprentice for his work used to go to the teacher. "The master shall teach him at his own home and

---

60. The Minor Law Books, p. 347, verse 9.
61. *Ibid*, p. 347, verse no. 10.
62. Samarāicca Kahā, p. 78.

feed. He must not employ him in work of a different description, and treat him like a son.

If one forsakes a master, who instructs him and whose character is unexceptionable, he may be compelled by forcible means to remain (at the master's house), and he deserves corporal punishment and confinement. Though his course of instruction be completed, an apprentice must continue to reside at the house of his master, till the fixed period has expired. The profit of whatever work he may be doing there belongs to his master."[63] This last point coincides with the basic philosophy of the modern "Wardha scheme" movement which includes in its curricula academic and practical courses of studies to make the pupils self-supporting. The plan further escheats the earning of the scholars to the school fund in the manner advocated by Manu.

Even after the completion of his courses of studies, the apprentice had to reside at the house of his master for the stipulated period. The profit earned by him through his work would go to the pocket of the master. A strict examination would be followed by the payment of the honorarium to the teacher.[64] The use of text-books in learning trade[65] was in vogue very much as it is in modern schools.

Our brief discussion of vocational education during the Jaina period reveals to us the fact that the Jaina fathers were conscious of the influence of geographical factors on the origin and distribution of various vocations, which is surprisingly modern. They also knew full well, along with the Hindu and Buddhist writers, the needs of adjusting vocations to the physical, emotional and physiological needs of the applicants seeking vocational training. The candidates for vocations were given a systematic and thorough vocational and educational guidance by the city-supervisors in an open conference in co-operation with the parents and the citizens. The opinion of the candidates was also respectfully taken into account. In vocational and educational selection, the parents also carefully took into account the relative influences of vocations on the physiology of their sons as also their respective merits and demerits and future prospect.

---

63. The Minor Law Books, pp. 133-134, verse nos. 17–19.
64. *Ibid,* p. 134, verse no. 120.
65. Prabandhacintāmaṇi, p. 104.

The Family, the Church, the School, the State and Industry—the five great institutions of society played an important role in imparting vocational education to the future citizens. Especially the state and industry co-operated in closer harmony in the enterprise. State interference in industry and its occupations is great and tremendous. The state introduced agricultural, industrial, and commercial pursuits under the direct control of Ṛṣabha, then Lord of Vinitā (Mod.Oudh), the first Jaina Tīrthaṅkara. We also know from the Buddhist and the Hindu sources something about guilds or associations of merchants which undertook to supervise and direct agriculture, trade, industry and commercial education in the country. For these, various departments were introduced in the association of the merchants, each under a specialist and the association constantly kept the people informed about economic activities of the country and occupational opportunities through its advisors. The association may appropriately be compared to a modern Board for Vocational Education. It must have under its control various trade-masters instructing their apprentices in their respective arts. The Board or Association was an independent organization under the general control of the state, enjoying full autonomy, imparting instruction in agricultural, technical, industrial and commercial courses subject to the restrictions set up by the State. Hence vocational education was both theoretical and practical, it applied theory to practice. The students could learn while earning though the profits went into the fund of their teachers. Besides, they learnt their trades under the direction of experts in an ideal occupational environment, and there was proper coordination between the instruction in the organized classes and the practical work in the factory or the farm and the vocations were carefully selected according to the natural bent of mind of the students.

## LECTURE IX.

# THE RELIGIOUS AND CULTURAL ACTIVITIES OF THE JAINA FATHERS.

It is a historical fact that all the Jaina prophets from Ṛṣabha to Mahāvīra addressed themselves directly to the masses in homely vernacular illustrating their sublime lessons with simple examples, parables and short stories. Theirs was the mission of uplifting the humble humanity in the sphere of religion. The missionary activities of the Jainas, like those of their Buddhist contemporaries were eminently practical. They were calculated to appeal more to the emotion than to the intellect of the audience. Religion is after all "morality touched with emotion" as Mathew Arnold has profoundly observed.

The sacred literature of the Jainas is embodied in the Canonical books known as the Aṅgas, twelve in number, which were put in shapes of books in order to assist the frail memory of man long after the demise of Lord Mahāvīra.[1]

It was first done two generations after the passing away of Mahāvīra and again the process had to be revived in the fifth century A.D. We may repeat here the well-known fact—that the Jainas are divided into two important sects—the Śvetāmbaras and the Digambaras—those who are clothed in white and those who go about naked. The last has a significance which must not be missed—the practice of nudity symbolizes absolute detestment from all worldly concerns. The Digambaras and the Śvetāmbaras do not agree in the details of their Faith. Into the details of the sectarian controversy we need not enter. Suffice it to say that during the earlier period of their history the Jainas were exclusively a religious body having nothing whatever to do with politics of the material world. Under pressure of circumstances into the details of which we need not enter, they were compelled to participate in politics, and in the tenth century A.D. they began to do so effectively

1. Maurice Winternitz, Ph.D., Vol. II, tr. by Mrs. S. Ketkar & Miss. H. Vohn, p. 432.

by capturing the control of the education of the princes from the hands of the Brāhmins.

It is well-known that when Jainism declined as a religion in the eastern part of India, it flourished in the West and the South owing to the effectiveness of teaching and the high standard of moral character of the Jaina missionaries, who easily overcame the opposition of their Brahmin rivals in the same field. The latter-day Jaina scholars imbibed a taste for secular culture and they made solid contributions to various fine-arts, philosophy and secular sciences. There are two distinct phases of cultural history of the Jainas—the early phase or the phase of Reformation and the later phase—the phase of Renaissance. The earlier phase was purely religious directed against ritualism, sacerdotalism, and dogmatism of the Vedas ; the later phase represented a combination of intellectual and physical culture represented by a host of sciences—viz. physiology, psychology, astronomy, astrology, mathematics, geography and other subjects. Let us proceed now to offer the audience a little more detailed account of the preaching tours of some of the Tīrthaṅkaras starting with Ṛṣabha.

Fittingly enough let us start with the first Tīrthaṅkara, Lord Ṛṣabha, who was born of a royal family, his father being king Navi of Oudh and his mother Merudevī[2]. The atmosphere surrounding his childhood was favourable to the mental and spiritual development of the child, who in course of time developed into a full-flelged religious reformer. Ṛṣabha seems to have received the ideal education for a prince ; he was happily married to the royal princesses Yaśavai and Sunandā, daughters of the kings of Kacca and Mahākacca[3] and when the proper time came he became the ruler of the land—he ruled it and ruled it well.

Soon after he realised the transitoriness of material pleasures and renounced the world and pursued his spiritual mission, being bent on the attainment of Kevalijñāna of perfect knowledge which is the sole source of salvation. In connection with this transition in his life a picturesque story of a heavenly damsel of the name of Nilamjasā trying to charm him by her attractive dance and herself being withered

2. Puṣpadanta, Mahāpurāṇa, edited by P. L. Vaidya, p. 600.
3. *Ibid*, p. 602.

away in the process is related.[4] The first converts of Ṛṣabha were Bambi and Sundarī and Suyakitti and Piyaṃvaya.[5]

In course of his teaching the first of the Tīrthaṅkaras taught his audience not only the elements of morality but also the rudimentary principles of science, physiology, psychology, astronomy and geography.[6] The other Tīrthaṅkaras followed in the foot-steps of the pioneer till we come to Mahāvīra, the last of the Tīrthaṅkaras.

Mahāvīra came of the royal family of Kuṇḍapura or Vaiśālī, his father being Siddhārtha, king of the land. He received a thoroughly perfect education becoming a royal prince in the Art-school as well as in the Institutions of higher learning. The courses of his studies embraced the various arts, the Vedas together with their aṅgas and the whole range of Brahmanical learning.

He renounced the world at the early age of twenty-eight with the consent of his father and pursued a career of spiritual conquest of truth. For twelve years he led a life of severe austerities and penance. It is at this stage of his life that he adopted the practice of going naked. After twelve years of spiritual discipline and austerity he attained to Kevalinship or perfect knowledge. Thereafter as Jacobi says 'He was recognized as omniscient, as a prophet of the Jainas or a Tīrthaṅkara (founder of the path) and had the title Jina (spiritual conqueror), Mahāvīra (a great hero), etc., which were also given to Śākyamuni. The last thirty years of his life he passed in teaching his religious system, and organized his Order of ascetics, which, as we have seen above was patronised or countenanced chiefly by those princes with whom he was related through his mother."[7] From the Atmānuśāsana, we learn that Mahāvīra had four names altogether. "That last Tīrthaṅkara Mahāvīra Svāmin is often referred to by four other names, Vīra, Vardhamāna, Ati-vīra, and Sanmati."[8] He was known among the Buddhists by the name of Nigaṇṭha Nātaputta.[9] His followers were drawn

4. Mahāpurāṇa, pp. 606, 610.
5. *Ibid,* p. 167.
6. *Ibid,* pp. 6161617.
7. Jacobi, Sacred Book of the East, pp. 15, 217.
8. Shri Guna Bhadra Ācārya, Ātmānuśāsana, tr. by Rai Bahadur J. L. Jaini, M.A., Bar-at-Law, p. I.
9. Maurice Winternitz, vol. II, p. 424.

chiefly from the Kṣatriya aristocracy and organized them into a community with lay members drawn from both the sexes. With Mahāvīra, the race of Jaina prophets or Tīrthaṅkara comes to an end.

From the materials at our disposal, we are neither in a position to assign the dates of the different stages of the missionary activities of of Mahāvīra not to identify with precision the different towns and cities he visited. All that we know definitely is that the area of his travels is very extensive embracing the whole of India from the Bay of Bengal to the Arabian sea. From the account given below we get firstly an approximate idea of the dimensions of his travels. We do not exactly know when or whence he started his spiritual tour. But the cities he visited may be thus arranged on the approximate contiguity of geographical locations. It may be added that some of the cities he visited have not yet been identified. Thus beginning from Campaka in Aṅga, he made his parepatetic tours and traversed through Rājagṛha, Nālandā, Mithilā, Vaiśālī, Benares, Alambhika, Kampilla, Śrāvastī, Panitabhūmi, Polāśapura, Vardhamāna (Guzerat), Astigrāma, etc.[10] In addition to the above cities Lord Mahāvīrā visited Bhadrika, Sāhanjani, Pāḍalasanḍa, Soriyapura, Rohida, Hastināpura, Usabhapura, Virapura, Parimatala city.[11] He made lay-converts and disciples in the Jaina monasteries located in the following important cities:—(1) Kāmadeva at Puṇṇabhaḍḍe sanctuary, in the suburb of Campaka,[12] (2) Vijaya at Rājagṛha,[13] (3) a Brahmin, Bāhula, at Kollaga, suburb of Śrāvastī,[14] (4) Ānanda of Vaṇijagrāma at Dūipalasa monastery in the same city[15] (5) Chulaṇipiya at Kotthaga monastery, in the suburb of Benares.[16] (6) Chullasayaga inn the garden of Sankhavāna in the suburb of Ābabhiya,[17] (7) Kuṇḍakoliya in the garden of Sahassambhavaṇa in

---

10a. Jaina Sūtras, part I, p. 264.
10b. Kalpa Sūtra And Nava Tattva, p. 91.
11. Vivagasuyam, pp. 1-132.
12. The Uvāsagadasāo, vol. II, pp. 64, 81, 85.
13. *Ibid,* appendix i, p. 1.
14. *Ibid,* p. 2.
15. *Ibid,* vol, II, pp. 9-10.
16. *Ibid,* p. 90.
17. *Ibid,* p. 103.

the suburb of Kampillapura.[18] In addition to the above list of wealthy lay disciples the Lord reluctantly admitted into his Order Gosāla[19] at Paniyabhūmi who like Devadatta proved hostile to his master and was expelled from the Order. Queen Nandā,[20] wife of Bimbisāra was admitted by the Lord into his ascetic fold at the Gunisila monastery at Rājagṛha (see lecture no. V).

Thus everywhere he was warmly received and enthusiastically greeted and a vast number of people of all ranks and of both sexes became his converts (see statistical table at the end of lecture no. IV). Mahāvīra the last of the Tīrthaṅkaras discharged supremely a synthetic mission by assimilating the teachings of his predecessors and by giving it a final form. He contributed towards the organization of the church and laid minor rules and regulations without which an organization cannot go. There was room in his fold both for monks and laymen.

Let us now proceed to offer a brief account of the intellectual activities of the Jainas in different branches of secular knowledge which so to say represent Jaina Renaissance. It was the necessary out-come of the Jaina system of education described in our pevious lectures. The Jaina Renaissance may be said to be the outcome of the Jaina Reformation by which we mean the vast and varied movement associated with the names of the Tīrthaṅkaras from Ṛṣabha downwards:

(1) Philosophy :—

Our theme namely the Jaina educational system has not directly much to do with the Jaina system of philosophy which is so very deep, rich and subtle. But it undoubtedly influenced its educational doctrine. The pluralistic realism of the Jainas with its peculiarly minute logic, elaborate psychology and sublime ethical code must have exerted a powerful influence on the enunciation of their educational philosophy.

(2) Religion:—

Jainism is a distinct religion having a distinct entity of its own. It is a combination of metaphysics, psychology, and what is popularly

18. *Ibid,* p. 106.
19. *Ibid,* appendix i, p. 2.
20. *Ibid,* vol. II, p. 97.

known as religion. Through sheer of ignorance and perverseness many western scholars like Barth regarded Jainism as a mere variation of Buddhism [21]. There are remarkable points of difference between the creeds as well as resemblance. Jainism admits the immortality of the soul while Buddhism denies its existence altogether. The Jaina system of philosophy is a type of dualism recognizing the existence of matter and soul while both are unreal with the Buddhists. The Jainism carries the doctrine of Ahiṁsā to a greater logical precision than what Buddhism does. Jainism reconciles itself to the institution of caste from which Buddhism totally departs.

(3) Art :—

There was nothing very original about the Jaina architecture but the Jainas were great builders devoting a good deal of care, attention and money towards the enrichment of their cities with buildings and towards the construction of temples of various designs and sizes in different places. The following extract from Vincent Smith gives us an idea of the nature of Jaina architecture. "In the domain of art the most notable achievements of the Jainas are the exquisite marble temples of Mount Abu, built in the local 'Guzerat' style. The Jaina temples in Mysore almost equally ornate in a different fashion. A peculiarity of Jain architecture is the massing of an enormous crowd of temples into a confined space, as at Palitana in Kathiawar and other places. The individual buildings are in the style of their age and locality."[22] The Jainas, it goes without saying thoroughly assimilated the Hindu and the Buddhistic[32] ideals and they in their turn greatly moulded the style of Muslim architecture in Guzerat.[24]

(4) Literature :—

Jaina literature is characterized by a severe tone of asceticism and unworldliness as contrasted with the graceful humanity of the Buddhist text. The early phase of the Jaina literature which was almost exclusively written in Prakrit dialects like Ardhamāgadhi and Mahārāstri possesses a philological interest of its own. It was from approximately

---

21. Sir S. Radhakrishnan, The Indian Philosophy, vol. I, pp. 290-291.
22. Vincent Smith, p. 11.
23. *Ibid,* p. 9,
24. *Ibid,* p. 32.

about the middle of the 8th century A.D. that Sanskrit came to be used for literary purpose by the Jainas of both the Śvetāmbara and the Digambara sects—the Śvetāmbara began to use it in the eighth century A.D. and the Digambara somewhat earlier. The Jaina sanskrit writers wrote in a variety of styles noted for purity and grace ; and in the tenth century A.D. they began to fall back upon the natural dialects of the people. In modern times the Jaina writers, quite in harmony with the spirit of age have begun to compose treatises in Guzerati, Tamil, Kanarese and Hindi thereby contributing to the enrichment of these literatures.[25]

Coming from the manner to the matter of Jaina literature we find that the Jainas much more thoroughly than the Buddhists mastered Hindu thoughts, sentiments and legends and adapted them to their own use. As for example the Kṛṣṇa cult and the legend of Draupaī appear in their Jaina version to the great edification of the readers belonging to the rank of the people. As an example to the point we may refer to the Prakrit Epic Pauma-cariyam (Padma Carita) by poet Vimala Sūri (330 years after the demise of Lord Mahāvīra).

It is to the credit of the Jainas that they immensely contributed to the Indian stock of knowledge not only in the fields of philosophy, art, religion and literature but also in the domain of secular knowledge like astronomy, astrology, mathematics, grammar, lexicography, poetics, and politics.[26]

Among the important Jaina mathematicians we must mention the name of Mahāvīrācārya,[27] a ninth century south Indian scholar who applied mathematics to the study of astronomy and regarded the knowledge of this science essential for the salvation of the soul. He absorbed the scientific ideals of the Hindu authority Brahma Gupta. His monumental work Ganitasārasaṃgraha was widely appreciated in south India and it was translated into Telugu language. Very releventlyy we may insert here a modern authoritative estimate of the contributions of these ancient worthies. "The so called Jaina operation (page 209) is akin to work found in Brahmagupta, and yet none of the problems

25. Maurice Winternitz, A History of Indian Literature, vol. II, p. 427.

26. *Ibid,* p.595.

27. Mahāvīrācārya, Gaṇita-Sāra--Sangraha, tr. by M. Raṅgācārya, M.A., Rai Bahadur.

is the same. The shadow problems, primitive cases of trigonometry and gnomonics, suggest a similarity among these three great writers, and yet those of Mahāvīrācārya are much better than the one to be found in either Brahmagupta or Bhāskara, and no questions are duplicated."[28] And we quote again. "His labours have revealed to the world a writer almost unknown to European scholars, and a work that is in many respects the most scholarly of any to be found in Indian mathematical literature."[29]

In connection with Jaina contributions to grammar, we must mention the name of Hemacandra, the great Jaina scholar of the eleventh century who on account of his vast erudition and versatile genius enjoyed the patrange of Siddharāja at whose request he composed his famous treatise on grammar known "Siddha Hemacandra" which was extensively circulated all over India and beyond.[30] Over and above. Hemacandra also wrote a commentary on his own grammar. He also composed Abhidhānacintāmaṇi and Anekārthasaṁgraha and other innumerable works of great merit.[31] Hemacandra was greatly influenced by his Hindu predecessors in his writings on grammar, metrics and poetics but he also added original element of his own. His Siddha-Hemacandra is clearly an imitation of Pāṇini's grammar but his chapters on Prakrit dialects are really original contributions. He wrote his secular works during the reign of Siddharāja and his religious works in the reign of Kumārapala,[32] of Guzerat, his patron.

(5) History :—

The Jaina writers wrote extensively on history, and their notable contributions being *Prabandhas* on diverse topics and Merutanga Ācārya's Prabandhacintāmaṇi gives us valuable information regarding the social, political, economical and educational conditions of his time. Forbes largely derived his source materials from this work for his *Rasamala*. The Jainas occasionally interferred in politics. The great author Hemacandra to whom we have already referred was, besides being many things, something also of a politician. Kalāka Sūri, a Jaina

28. Mahāvīrācārya, Op. Cit. p. xxii.
29. *Ibid*, p. xxiv.
30. Dr. G. Bühler, Life of Hemacandra, pp. 15-16.
31. Hemacandra, Kumārapālacarita, pp. xxiv-xxv. edited by Dhruva.

monk took part in politics and he also once led an army against the king of Ujjain.

During the latter part of this lecture we have mainly dwelt upon the intellectual activities of the Jainas which may be said to have constituted a period of Renaissance which is associated with its development of literature, secular arts and sciences. Its earlier part has mainly dealt with religious activities which may be said to have represented the Reformation movement. History does not always repeat itself after all. In European history the Renaissance movement preceded the Reformation movement. Here the order was reversed. What we have designated as the Jaina Reformation was associated with religion and philosophy. We have discussed religion somewhat in detail but we have refrained from dwelling on philosophy almost altogether because of want of space.

# LECTURE X

## CONCLUSION

Friends,

We propose to present you in this, the last lecture of the series with a résumé of the nine lectures already delivered and nothing more. The family has been from the very start, both a biological and a cultural institution. It was the earliest form of school, imparting education for the cultural uplift of humanity. In course of time, with the growth of the complexities of civilization, it came to be superseded by the organized school. From the earliest times, the school was almost invariably associated with the church as an agency of education. In course of time the latter absorbed the former altogether. It was so in Europe. It was almost so here in India. The Brahmins used to control both the secular and the religious education of the land.

In the second lecture, we noticed how the Vedic and the Art-schools came into being as two distinct institutions—the former exclusively for the twice-born, and the latter for the Śūdras and other members of the lower order in society, though the twice-born too could join it, if they would. There were no proper articulation between these two grades of institutions ; and they were running into parallel directions without meeting at any common point. The attendance in the former institutions was compulsory for the twice-born especially for the Brahmins ; but they had the option to join the latter, and this option depended on the postponement of the *upanayana* ceremony according to Gṛhya-Sūtrās.

This proves conclusively that the Brahmins might easily join the art-school. The curricula in the Vedic school was encyclopaedic, embracing purely academic and scientific courses of studies meant for the twice-born as a preparation for their multifarious duties or vocations of life. Physical education was not neglected. Early-rising, collection of faggots and other manual work done for their teachers assisted in an informal way the physical training of the alumni of the Vedic schools. The Brahmanic curricula offered facilities for mental development of the scholars. These were framed on sound psychological and sociological principles—and were not forced upon all regardless of the mental differences of the recepients. According to Manu, the twice-born scholars were given the latitude to drop out after 36,18 and 9 years of study of the three Vedas. Consequently, according to this scheme one might drop out of the Vedic school after 12,6 and 3 years of study. Only on rare occasions, brilliant scholars who dedicated their lives to the cause of learning, devoted themselves to the study of the whole range of the four Vedas extending to 48 years according to the Smṛti. It is quite likely that the scholars of average intelligence and modest ambition did not study the range of the encyclopaedic courses of Vedic studies.

The Kṣatriyas, necessarily, paid scanty attention to the study of the Vedas devoting their serious care to solid, positive and practical sciences such as politics, science of tactics, physical education, painting, music and languages as a preparation for their life's calling. The Vaiśyas, likewise, reserved their serious care for the study of the practical arts and sciences with special reference to varta-śāstras, agriculture, cattle-raising, commerce, trade, and industry. Naturally, these two groups of scholars spent their minimum time in the Vedic school with a special stress on the course of studies required for their vocations. Briefly speaking, the curricula in the Brahmanic school were remarkably adjusted to the mental and social needs of the scholars and the courses were more philosophical and less practical for the Brahmins and more practical and less philosophical for the Kṣatriyas and the Vaiśyas. In other words, personality and society were the standards of education. The Brahmanic education was carefully designed to preserve the then political and social structure of the country—i.e. education was framed after the pattern of the state. It is patent that the Vedic educaion took a thorough account of the facts of human nature ; it had its basis in the very psychology of man as a practical, positive being whose education to be of any good, must not be an *airy* nothing, but a real help, guiding him onward and forward to the path of self-realisation through self-elevation. Then again, it was thoroughly alive to the important economic principle of the Division of Labour, which was really at the root of the institution of caste—an institution with which the educational philosophy of India was so integrally connected.

The lecture method was fully utilized, though individual instruction too was in vogue. The corporate life was brisk. The spirit of association was vigorous. The teachers were organized under pariṣads, resembling the Mediaeval European universities offering instructions to students—both religious and secular. There was a hierarchy of officers discharging their respective duties. Reference to Pariṣads or Brahman Sabhas is made in the Kāvyamimāṁśa of Rājaśekhara. These Pariṣads used to hold examinations in which learned scholars of those days of hoary antiquity used to sit. This practice establishes beyond doubt its academic character. Education was no play in ancient India. There was no saturnalia of option and looseness. It was a slow, sure, stern and steady discipline of the mind needing practice, devotion, and care.

The proper articulation between the Vedic and the art-school was gradual. The parallel system of organization was replaced by the ladder-scheme during the time of Lord Buddha who joined the writing or the art-school as preparatory to joining Taxila University where he mastered the whole range of learning available in his days, and thus became perfectly fit for the discharge of his royal duties.

The movement for this articulation between the Vedic and the art-school reached its culmination, when these institutions were controlled by the Jaina fathers. Their monasteries, as a result of this assimilation of culture of their won, assumed a cosmopolitan nature, imparting instruction in a vast range of subjects. Specialization went hand to hand with liberalism in their realm of studies. Their institutions of learning became a melting-pot of cultures as it were, thus exerting a tremendous influence on the mental, moral and political life in India. The Jaina fathers had a remarkable power of adaptability ; and to make their institutions of learning very popular, they tactfully incorporated the diverse types of cultures in their monastic universities.

Like the Vedic or the Brahmanic schools, the encyclopaedic curricula of the Jainas took into account the psychologcial and the sociological factors in framing their courses of studies. That is "child-life" and "Social-institutions" became the standards of education. Naturally, in the monastic schools of the Jainas, there were ecclesiastical and secular departments offering instruction in the Brahmanic, the Buddhistic learning and in the Arts and the Aṅgas of the Jainas. The Jaina fathers had a wonderful grasp of geography the knowledge of which they utilized in founding the monasteries.

Thus, they always like the Buddhist fathers, selected sites for their monasteries and the nunneries in the suburbs of the capital cities, commercial towns—inland or coastal—and they were always careful in taking into account the geographical factors of the locality—their location within the vicinity of the highways and byeways, natural scenery surcharged with fragrant breezes of the lotous-pools, the humming of bees, sweet-chirping of various species of birds, and temperate climate devoid of disturbing elements—natural or artificial.

The Jaina monasteries were well organized under a hierarchy of officers such as Presidents, Ācāryas, Upādhyāyas, Śramaṇas, Pravajyādāyakas, Niryāpakas and other officers and teachers required to conduct both the systems of administration and instruction obtaining therein ; and they became important centres of culture and learning, attracting lay scholars from all ranks in society.

.No tution feess were charged from lay scholars who were even given free room and board in case of necessity. Moral discipline was strictly enforced upon all, especially upon the novices who were subjected to rules of asceticism ; and their courses of studies included the Aṅgas as well as sacred and secular texts. All the Jaina monasteries taught the novices their eleven Aṅgas at the least; and we have constant references to the practice in sacred texts. Seventy-two arts are mentioned in the Prabandhakoṣa as the curricula prescribed for the education of Bappa Bhaṭṭi and prince Āma by Siddhasena Sūri at the Jaina monastery at Moḍerapura in the province of Guzerat.

The Jaina fathers introduced an ethical code governing the daily programme of the monks—physical, mental and moral. At least three hours' daily study of the Jaina scriptures was strictly enjoined upon Jaina monks and nuns, the violation of which was looked upon with grave concern. They enjoined begging-tours upon all monks similar to the practice that was in vogue in the Vedic or the Brahmanic schools with this difference that the former used to beg alms from all classes of citizens from the rich to the poor without any reservation.

The Jaina monasteries had excellent libraries or Bhāṇḍāras attached to them where competent and highly educated monks spent their time in studing, and copying sacred books, and writing books on diverse subjects. In brief, the Jaina Bhāṇḍaras like the Mediaeval European libraries, were rich depositories of Indian literatures on diverse subjects from the religious to the secular. They exerted a profound influence on the mental and moral uplift of the Indian people.

Nunneries were also founded in the cities for the spread of education among the women, especially among the nuns and the female novices. The Jaina fathers were very liberal; and readily admitted women into their fold. The nunneries acquired popularity and ladies from the royal household, especially the royal consorts voluntarily joined them. The female novices were admitted into the Jaina order before the assembly of the monks ; and after their formal admission they were handed over to the nun-in-charge, under whose guidance they received training in the eleven Aṅgas of the Jainas as preparatory to their religious career. The nuns were chiefly instrumental in the spread of education among the fair sex. The nuns imparted instruction also to female lay scholars in religion and moral precepts attending their classes from their home. We learn from the Kathākoṣa that princess of the royal family of Gangapura received religious instruction regularly from the abbess Chandrayacas of the same city.[1] The Jaina nuns received all–round training in diverse subjects—both religious and secular and we have on record the cases of Bhadda and Nanduttara, the Jaina nuns who challenged Sariputra and Moggallana the two apostles of Lord Buddha in open debates on points of religion. Though both these nuns could not stand the debates, yet it was a glorious defeat for them both. We do not have any evidence to prove if the Jaina nuns could be elevated to the coveted position of an Arhat ; but they were promoted to the position of the head of a community of nuns under the charge of a Tīrthaṅkara. Thus Brāhmī-sundarī, Arya Yakṣīnī, Puspakula, Candrabālā and Salasa Revatī were eminent Jaina nuns who rose to the position of a head of community of nuns and lay votaries respectively under Ṛṣabha, Aristanemi, Pārśva and Mahāvīra.

Education was imparted to lay females desiring to enter into domestic duties in the family, state and the schools. We have noticed above

---

1. Kathākoṣa, p. 116.

how the Jaina Church also undertook to train the lay females in religion. Our knowledge of the responsibility of the Church in imparting the secular education to the lay female scholars is very defective. In the family, the state and the school the female lay scholars studied the whole range of encyclopaedic curricula prescribed for the Art-school. Their courses of studies were admirably fitted to their physical, emotional and mental growth. Emphasis was laid upon the personality of the pupils, their special aptitudes, interests, native abilities, and social conditions in giving them the best kind of education as a preparation for their domestic and civic duties. Thus, fine Arts took care of their physical, emotional and mental needs ; and the academic or literary courses including the Vedic courses and the classical languages took note of their intellectual appetite. In addition to these needs the needs of society were also taken into account. Briefly speaking, as in the monastic school "Child-life" and "Society" were the standard of education. The female scholars were made to study seventy-two arts of the Jainas with a 'specialization' in the subject of their choice. The courses were organized with a view to fit into the nature and specific abilities of the scholars. Thus rigid courses of studies were not forced upon all scholars regardless of their abilities, tastes, aptitudes and natural bent of mind.

The females also received higher education in the Vedic or the Brahmanic school. Female education was not restricted to a particular community, but females of all ranks—Brahmins, Kṣatriyas, Vaiśyas and even adult female cooks could receive the benefit of higher education. Diploma of Paṇḍitā was conferred upon successful candidates. After completing their courses of studies, they found employment in various vocations and even a princess of Bhoja engaged herself as a scribe in copying the Jaina texts.

The Art-schools were very popular and they were prevalent in the capital cities, commercial towns and even in the distant regions of the country.

On the education of the princess or the guardians of state, the influence of the family, the church, the state, and the school was immense. The education of the princes began from the prenatal stage to their adolescence and post-adolescence and education was carefully planned and adjusted to the growing needs of the growing child. In the prenatal stage, special care was taken of the mother, her diet was regulated and her environment was made comfortable and ideal, and disturbing elements were removed.

After birth they were left to the charge of groups of female nurses especially trained in child-care and they with their special skill assisted in the mental, moral and physical well-being of the child. We pointed out in course of our lectures how the female nurses were versed in fine arts, and in higher education and some of them had Paṇḍitā' prefixed to their names—more as a scholastic stamp than a mere surname. For such Paṇḍitā nurses showed their skill in drawing pictures and were skilled in literatures and sacred lores and were constant companions of their masters' children on terms of equality. Adolescent princesses had such Paṇḍitā nurses as their companions.

The formal education of the royal princess did not begin till their seventh birthday or eighth year from conception when they were sent to the art-schools to receive instruction in the seventy-two arts comprising 3 R's, vernacular languages, fine-arts, sciences both physical and military. The Jainas included the Vedas and the Vedaṅgas in the art-curricula of the monasteries. In some cases as in Vinita (Mod. Oudh) in the family of Ṛṣabha the young princes and the princesses received their education in the arts and the sciences at the palace from Bharata the son of Ṛṣabha, the Lord of Vinitā.

It is clear that the female education in Jaina India was more scientific, practical, and efficient than the so called female education of modern civilization. This is merely a perverted type of male education. That was a genuine type of mental discipline meant to secure a practical purpose, calculated to make women real and solid builders of civilization and culture. A comparative glance at the achievements of each type will convince anybody of the truth of our assertion.

The princes also received their education in the Jaina monasteries in the seventy-two arts as a preparation for their royal duties. We already noticed how prince Āma of Kanouj, son of King Yaśovarman received his education in the seventy-two arts along with Bappa Bhaṭṭi from Siddhasena at Moḍerapura in the kingdom of Guzerat. The Jaina fathers in the west and in the south of India captured the educational control of the princes as a measure of increasing their influence

16

and power in the current politics of the day. In this object they succeeded pre-eminently.

The Art-school quite independent of the monasteries imparted instruction to princes and other lay-scholars in the seventy-two arts. The curricula in the art-schools were carefully organized on sound psychologial and sociological basis and the teaching in the school was vitally related to the realities of life.

The state also co-operated with the art-school in imparting instruction to its alumuni. Especially in the education of the princes the supervision of the State is clearly perceptible., We learn from the "Romantic Legend of Śākya Buddha" how king Śuddhodana, the father of Lord Buddha held formal conference with his ministers and how in consulation with them he appointed specialists—Viśvāmitra to train young Siddhārtha in 3 R's and fine-arts and Khāntadeva to train the young prince in physical and military sciences. For physical and military training especially prepared spacious fields were set up in the suburbs of cities for practical training. The group and individual instructions were known. The physical and military education preceded the academic and the fine-art classes in the art-school. Special training-grounds for horse-riding must have been used, as it is definitely learned from the Jaina literature. The education of the princes was based on sound psychological principles and proper balance was maintained between the mind and the body and both the theoretical and the practical education was carried on simultaneously. Sometimes the students of military sciences made demonstration of their skill in the use of the various implements of warfare. This resembles the modern performance test as demanded of applicants for admission into vocational or trade schools.

The influence of the State in the education of the prince was especially felt in the education of the adult king. Thus king Kumārapāla of Guzerat who had a chequered career, hired a private tutor to train him in his palace after dinner. Gradually he mastered the 3 R's, literatures, politics and other sciences and arts demanded of a king.

The Art-school, as remarked before, existed in all the important cities, towns and in distant regions of the Indian peninsula. It is a very ancient institution incidentally referred to by Manu and Bṛhaspati as an educational institution meant for the non-Brahmins. But gradually it came to be a popular institution attended even by Brahmin scholars, for we have ample evidences in the Kathāsarit sāgara to prove that the Brahmins excelled others in fine arts and military sciences. We learn from the Mahābhārata also that Droṇācārya was thoroughly versed in the military sciences.

The contribution of the Jaina fathers to geography was immense as we noticed before. Their knowledge of geography was sound judged by the standard of those days and they very well realized the influence of geographical factors on the origin of vocations—a fact which is very modern. In our lecture on vocational education of the Jainas we tried to trace the influence of the geographical factors, viz. location, mountains and reliefs, water–inland bodies of water and oceanic water, soil, climate, minerals and transportation system on the origin of vocations. We have discovered the influence of the geographical factors on various vocations to be inseparable. Vocations differ in diverse regions because they are conditioned by the geographical factors. Thus vocations in the plains are bound to be quite different from those of the hilly regions. The vocations on the coastal cities are again different from those in the inland cities.

Next we discussed the application of psychological principles to vocational selection. In ancient times caste system was the criterion of vocational and educational selections. The individual was made subservient to the static society. Gradually and steadily as a result of agitation made by the Buddhists and Jainas the antiquated practice was supplanted by sound psychological basis of vocational and educational guidance. Systematic vocational guidance in consultation with the parents, citizens and the city-supervisors of the morals of youths was made. No vocation was forced upon the unwilling mind. The parents made a careful survey of different vocations—their merits and demerits, their demand upon the native and the specific abilities and on the physiology of their sons. The working conditions, future prospect, monitary advantages and other factors were carefully considered before selecting the vocations for their sons. Native and specific abilities were especially considered to fit the right vocations for the right candidates. Briefly speaking, to eliminate mal-adjustment or labour-turn-over, vocations and their programmes of studies were carefully selected on a sure psychological basis after a careful study of the man and his vocation. This is a grand monument of the practical common foresight of our ancestors directed to the formulation of a sound scheme of education. Science and idealism here went hand in hand.

In vocational education the influence of the family, the church, the state, the school and industry—the five great institutions of society is clearly perceptible. These institutions especially the state and industry were chiefly instrumental in imparting vocational education to the mercantile communities, artizans, agriculturists and other workers in society. The state took a leading part in patronising vocational education. Assemblies of the merchants with departmental system and guild were organized, subject to the general control of the state. These were autonomous bodies with the right to make their own byelaws and with a hierarchy of officers to supervise the vocational education of the students. The Art-school also opened vocational classes. Vocational education was practically free and compulsory as we noticed in connection with our lecture on the subject. No scholar was allowed to drop out of the school before completion of the stipulated period. Its students like those of the Art-schools received theoretical and practical education simultaneously. They worked in the factories, ranches or in other places of work both for practical experience and monitary gain, and in the vocational class they received theoretical instruction on their selected occupations. Thus like the American Part-Time Co-Operative schools, the students of the vocational classes received both the theoretical and practical training at the same time.

Thus work and instruction were closely correlated and the pupils in the mercantile and guild schools used to receive training in commerce, business, industry, technology, agriculture and in other vocations of life in an occupational environment.

The activities of these above mentioned four institutions excepting the family were closely interrelated. The state was instrumental in the support of the Jaina religion and education and the industry of the country which again added to the national wealth.

Next we discussed the influence of the transportation system on the religious and educational activities of the Jaina fathers, i.e., the principal routes followed by the Jaina fathers, in their preaching tours and their consequent influence on the moral and mental life of the people. The debates held in the Jaina monasteries and the migration of the Jaina fathers from the different Jaina monasteries to participate in them contributed to the dissemination of the religious principles. Finally we have touched very briefly on the contribution of the Jaina fathers to religion, philosophy, literatures and sciences.

With this brief survey of our nine lectures, we may safely conclude that during the Jaina period, centuries before the Christian era down to the fourteenth century A.D., the Jaina fathers were busily active in the spread of their religion and culture among the people. Their education and preachings were based upon sound educational psychology and the Jaina fathers were thoroughly acquainted with the child psychology, adolescent psychology and educational psychology and their whole education was based upon sound psychological principles. Our study reveals the following pedagogical principles touching upon all aspects of education which are astonishingly modern. Our survey has given us a significant picture of an ancient civilization :

1. It appeared in course of our lectures that the Jaina system of education was a thoroughly comprehensive one meant for making its recepients good citizens, sound churchmen, and efficient rulers of the future, fit for discharging their tasks. All the four great agencies of education operated with this great end in view.

2. Secular education was segregated from the religious though both the types of education were imparted in the Jaina monasteries.

3. Education was controlled by the Family, the Church, the State, the School and Industry all co-ordinating with one another for a common cause.

4. The Jaina Church had a business council to settle dispute with the state or any other constituent body. It had an academic council or assembly of the learned monks entrusted with the task of the reception of the wandering Arhats, arrangement of extension lectures etc. It had under jurisdiction of these two organizations a hierarchy of teachers and officers each with specific duties in teaching, preaching, in initiating the novices before the Assembly of the monks and in rehabilitating the morally pervert. Here the strict administrative principle of authority and responsibility were strictly adhered to and each teacher and officer had his own responsibility and authority, the violation of which was not tolerated.

5. It conferred academic degrees such as Paṇḍitā, Bahuśruta and

Doctorate (Bhaṭṭa) upon the most successful and competent scholars. The last and the highest degree was conferred upon the thoroughly competent scholars noted for learning and originality in research.

6. The state aiso had a department of Education with the "Superior Paṇdita' as its head. This officer had the right even to expel a scholar from the country for a period of twelve years. It is also gathered from Buddhistic sources how the premier with his colleagues held a conference with king Śuddodhana of Kapilavāstu when summoned by him to select the best available teachers for the education of prince Siddrārtha. This proves that one of the ministers in the state was in charge of the portfolio of education in addition to his other responsibility much after the practice of modern governments. The state accorded its close co-operation to the great agencies of education by providing them with training-grounds for military exercise, parks for recreation and so forth. Education was distinctly a concern of the state.

7. The Brahmanic and the Art-schools flourished in the same city and the rigid practice of attending the former institution before admission into the latter was not universally followed by the twice-born.

8. The Jaina fathers made their monasteries a cosmopoliton institution of learning offering instructions on the Vedas, the Aṅgas, the Buddhistic Literature, etc., thus making their seminaries the melting-pots of culture.

9. Industry had Associations of its own. The merchants, the artizans and other workers were all organized under their own guilds which had their codes of ethics and bye-laws subject to their general approval of the state. The merchants' Association had jurisdiction over wider regions with various departments each under a specialist. The guilds according to Bṛhaspati must have supervisors. Sometimes commission was appointed by the king to assist the merchants.

10. The church, the school and industry enjoyed autonomy and the State intervened sparingly.

11 The Jaina educational systems, as described in the Jaina literature were based on sound psychology. The 'Self' and 'Society' were the two fundamental basis upon which the entire educational curricula were based. The psychological factors included physical, emotional

and mental and the curricula in the art-school or the art-courses in the Jaina monasteries were organized in such a way as to satisfy the physical urge of the young children of both the sexes. Physical education, military training, music and dancing were appropriate courses to take care of the motor activities so predominant in little children. The fine arts like painting and music which are eminently conducive to the development of the imaginative and emotional lives of their votaries were extensively utilized by the Jaina educators. We have given concrete examples of the practice in course of these lectures. This practice of imparting education with a view to the specific ability of the recipients was a sound one. It was followed by all the ancient authorities whether Hindu, Buddhistic or Jaina. The Hindu practice is concretely illustrated in the case of Mālavikā, the heroine of a drama by Kālidāsa ; reference to whom has already been made. The academic courses in the art-schools, comprehensive and perfect, as they were, supplied food to the mental appetite of advanced scholars. Briefly speaking the curricula were framed to fit them into the physical, mental and emotional traits of the scholars. Through an ideal curricula a proper balance between mind and body was maintained. This is evident from the very scheme of studies followed—a scheme of physical, mental and spiritual cultures.

12. Education—academic or vocational was never enforced upon the unwilling mind. Teaching was adjusted to the gradual growth of the mind, premium was placed upon native abilities and specific abilities and sex-bar was unknown and both the sexes pursued the same courses with specialization on the subject of their own choice. Performance test used to be administered before admitting students to military courses. In other words try-out courses were in vogue in Jaina and Buddhist India. The ancients knew full well the difference between general abilities and specific abilities and the curricula were adjusted according to this plan. All the seventy-two arts were not studied together. There must have been some kind of specialization even in those days of cosmopolitanism.

13. In the trade school the work and the instruction went on simultaneously thus each supplementing the other.

14. Adult education was in vogue in India as is evident from the writings of the Jaina fathers.

15. It was popular in this country among the people of all classes from the king to the humble folk.

16. It included 3 R's, literatures, politics, classical languages of Brahmanic cultures and the eleven Aṅgas of the Jainas.

17. The church, the state and the schools all worked in harmony in educating the illiterate adults. Extension lecture-tours in connection with the Jaina church were organized to spread culture and learning among the mass of both sexes. The state influence was especially felt in removing illiteracy even from the ruler.

We have thus discussed with you, gentlemen, in the course of these ten short lectures hurriedly prepared some of the outstanding educational theories and practices that were in vogue in ancient India from Ṛṣabha to that of Hemacandra, the last of the great Jaina scholars, a prolific writer on various subjects—religious and secular.

Any impartial critic will from the points enumerated above notice that all the fundamental educational aims and principles, were based on those psychological principles which are most modern—and which are the ground work of modern European and American pedagogy. It must be an agreeable surprise to see how our educational philosophy has been thoroughly assimilated by the Europeans and the Americans only to be re-exported to us through our learned pedagogues, the cultural ambassadors of their *alma meters.* Even superficial students know how the translation of the Indian classics–Sanskrit, Buddhistic and Jaina into European languages during the latter half of the eighteenth and the whole of the nineteenth centuries and onwards has placed the whole stock of the knowledge of our ancestors within the easy reach of the West. The East and the West have met together in the realm of culture, in the field of thought. Into various branches of learning, for good or evil, each has influenced the other. In the region of educational philosophy, with which we are especially concerned in these lectures, the westerners have borrowed a good deal from India directly, and consciously and it is to be regretted even without acknowledgment of the obligation.

# BIBLIOGRAPHY

## A. Original Jaina Sources.


1. The Antagaḍadasāo And Aṇuttarovavāiya-dasāo, tr. by L. D. Barnett, M.A., D.Litt. Printed and Published under the patronage of the Royal Asiatic Society, London.
2. Anuyogadvāra-Sūtram, Edited by Dr. D. G. Sanghani, H.L.M.S.
3. Ardha Māgadhī Reader, edited and tr. by Banarasi Das Jain, M.A. Published by The Punjab University, Lahore.
4. Atmānuśāsana, by Shri Guna Bhadra Ācārya, tr. by Rai Bahadur J. L. Jaini, M.A., Bar-at-Law. Assisted by Jaina Dharma Bhuṣaṇa Brahmacāri Sital Prasadji, Published by Pandit Ajit Prasad, M.A., LL.B. The Central Jaina Publishing House. Ajitashram, Lucknow.
5. Bṛhat Kalpasūtra And Original Niryukti, Edited by Guru Shri Chaturvijaya and his Śiṣya Punyavijaya. Published by Shri Ātmānanda Jain Sabhe, Bhavanagar.
6. Commentary of Uttarādhyāyana-Sūtram, part II, tr. by Charpentier. Archives D'Etudes Orientales, Publiees Par J. A. Lundell. Uppsala.
7. Gaṇitasāra-Saṁgraha, by Mahāvīrācārya. tr. by M. Rangācārya, M.A., Rao Bahadur. Published under the orders of the Government of Madras. Printed by The Superintendent, Government Press.
8. Gomatasāra, Jiva-Kunda, by Shri Nemichandra Siddhant Chakravorty. Assisted by Jaina Dharma Bhuṣaṇa Brahmacāri, Sital Prasadji. Published by Pandit Ajit Prasad, M.A., LL.B. The Central Jaina Publishing House. Ajitashram, Lucknow.
9. Jaina Jātaka Or Lord Ṛṣabha's Purvabhāvas, Being an English Translation Book I, of Hemacandra's Triṣaṣṭiśalākā-puruṣa-Caritra, tr. by Amulya Charan Vidyabhushana. Matilal Banarasi Das. The Punjab Sanskrit Books Depot. Lahore.
10. Jaina Sūtras, parts, I & II, tr. by. Hermann Jacobi. Oxford. At The Clarendon Press.
11. Kalpa-Sūtra And Nava Tattva, tr. by Rev. J. Stevenson, D.D., London. Printed for The Oriental Translation Fund of Great Britain And Ireland.
12. Karakanda Cāriu, by Muni Kanakamāra. Edited with introduction and tr. by Hiralal Jain, M.A., LL.B.,
13. Kathākoṣa, The, tr. by C. H. Tawney, M.A. Printed and Published under the patronage of the Royal Asiatic Society.
14. Kumārapālacarita, The (Prākṛta Dvyasraya Kāvya),—Hemacandra. Edited by Shankar Pandurang Pandit, M.A., D.Lit. Published by The Bhandarkar Oriental Research Institute, Poona.

15. Mahāpurāṇa, vol. I, Puṣpadanta, edited by P. L. Vaidya, M.A., (Cal) D.Litt (Paris).
Published by Mānikchand Digambara Jaina Granthamālā, Bombay,
16. Nirāyavalīyāo, Edited by A. S. Gopani, M.A., & V. J. Chokshi, B.A., Published by Sambhubhai Jagshi Shah, Gandhi Road, Ahmedabad.
17. Niyamasāra (The Perfect Law), by Shri Kundakunda Ācārya. tr. by Uggar Jain, M.A., LL.B.
Published by The Central Jaina Publishing House, Ajitashram, Lucknow.
18. Paūma-Chariyam, by Vimalā Sūri, Chapters, I-IV. tr. by B. A. Changule, M.A., and N. V. Vaidya, M.A.
19. Pravacana-Sāra, The, by Śrī Kundakundācārya, (Together with the commentary, Tattva dīpikā by Amṛtacandra Sūri) tr. by Barend Faddegon. Cambridge, at The University Press.
20. Pravacana-Sāra, The, by Śrī Kundakundācārya. Edited by A. N. Upadhye, M.A. Published by Shetha Manilal Revashankar Jhaveri. Bombay.
21. Padmānanda Mahākāvya, by Amaracandra Sūri. Edited by H. R. Kapadia, M.A. Baroda. Oriental Institute,
22. Paramātmā-prakāśā, The, by Sri Yogindra Ācārya. tr. by Rickhab Dass Jain, B.A., and Kumar Devendra Prasad. Arrah (India).
23. Prabandhakoṣa, Vol. I, by Rājaśekhara Sūri. Edited by Jina Vijaya. Published by The Adhisthata-Singhi Jaina Jnānapitha. Santiniketan.
24. Prabandhacintāmaṇi, by Merutuṅga Ācārya. tr. by C. H. Tawney, M.A. Calcutta. Published by the Asiatic Society.
25. Samarāicca-Kahā, by Haribhadra Sūri, (First Two Chapters), Edited and tr. by M. C. Modi, M.A., LL.B. Published by Sambhulal Jagshi Shah, Gandhi Road, Ahmedabad.
26. Sthavirāvalicarita, by Hemacandra. Edited by Hermann Jacobi, Ph.D. Calcutta, Published by The Asiatic Society.
27. Triṣaṣṭiśalākā-puruṣa-Caritra, Vols. I, II, Oriental Institute, Baroda.
28. Uvāsagadasāo, Vol. II, tr. by A. F. Rudolf, Ph.D. (Tubingen).
29. Vivagasuyam, (The Eleventh Aṅga of The Jaina Canon.) tr. by V. J. Chokshi, M.A., and M. C. Modi, M.A., LL.B. Published by Sambhubhai Pagshi Shah, Gurjar Grantha Karyalaya. Gandhi Road, Ahmedabad.
30. Yogaśāstra, Vol. I, by Hemacandra, (With the Commentary called Svopajnavivarana.) Calcutta : Published by The Asiatic Society.

B. Secondary Jaina Sources :—

1. Life And Stories of The Jaina Savior Parsvanatha, by Maurice Bloomfield. The Johns Hopkins Press.
2. Mediaeval Jainism (With special reference to the Vijayanagaram Empire.) by Bhasker Ananda Saletore, M.A., Ph.D. Karnataka Publishing House. Bombay.

C. Hindu Sources :—

1. Agnipuāṇam, Edited by Paṇḍitabara Pañcānana Tarkaratna. Calcutta. Printed and Published by Sri Natabara Chakravorty at the Bangabasi Press.

2. Arthaśāstra, by Cāṇakya, tr. by R. Shamasastry, B.A., Bangalore. Printed At The Government Press.

3. Bādarāyaṇa, The Vedanta Sūtras, tr. by Rai Bahadur Sris Chandra Vasu, Published by the Panini Office. Bhuvaneswari Asram, Bahadurganja. Allahabad.

4. Gṛhya Sūtras, (Rules of Vedic Domestic Ceremonies), part I, tr. by Hermann Oldenberg. Oxford. At the Clarendon Press.

5. Institute of Viṣṇu, tr. by Julius Jolly, Oxford. At the Clarendon Press.

6. Kathāsaritsāgara, Vol. I, tr. by C. H. Tawney, M.A. Calcutta. Printed by J. W. Thomas, At the Baptist Mission Press.

7. Kāvyamīmāṁsā, by Rājaśekhara, Edited by C. D. Dalal, M.A., and Anantakrishna Sastri. Published Under The Authority of the Government of His Highness the Mahāraja Gaekwad of Baroda Central Library, Baroda.

8. Laws of Manu, tr. by G. Bühler. Oxford. At the Clarendon Press.

9. Mahābhāratam, The, Edited by Haridas Siddhantavagis, from Siddhanta Vidyalaya.

10. Minor Law Books, part I, tr. by Julius Jolly. Oxford. At the Clarendon Press.

11. Mudrārākṣasa or The Signet Ring. By Visakha Datta. tr. by Prof. K. H. Dhruva, B.A., Second Edition. Poona. The Oriental Book Agency.

12. Nyāya Sūtras, Vol. II, (With the Bhāṣya of Vātsyāyana and The Vārtika of Uddyotakara) tr. by Mahāmahopādhyāya Ganganath Jha, M.A., D.Lit. Vol. II. Published by the Editor, 'Indian Thought', Allahabad.

13. Skandapūrāṇa, 4th Canto, Edited by Kalikrishna Mandal.

14. Śrīmatbhāgabatam, Edited by Brahmachari Nityasvarupa.

15. Tantravārtika, by Kumārila Bhaṭṭa ; tr. by Mahāmahopādhyāya Dr. Ganganath Jhā, M.A., D.Litt. Printed by The Baptist Mission Press. Vol. I to III. Published by The Asiatic Society of Bengal.

16. Test of a Man Being, The Puruṣa Parīkṣā, The, by Vidyāpati Thākura. tr. by Sir George A. Grierson, O.M., K.C.I.E. Royal Asiatic Society, London.

17. Vaikhānasasmārtasūtram, tr. by Dr. W. Caland. Printed At The Baptist Mission Press. Published by The Asiatic Society of Bengal, Calcutta.

18. Vikrama's Adventure, tr. by Franklin Edgerton, part I, Cambridge, Massachusetts, Harvard University Press. London, Humphrey Milford. Oxford University Press.

D. Secondary Hindu Sources :—

1. Indian Philosophy, The, by Sir S. Radhakrishnan, Vol. I, George Allen and Unwin Co.
2. A History of Pre-Buddhistic Indian Philosophy, by Dr. B. M. Barua.

E. Original Buddhist Sources :—

1. Aṅguttara Nikāya (Gradual Sayings), Vol. II. tr. by F. L. Woodward, M.A. London. Published for The Pali Text Society, by The Oxford University Press. Amen House, And at New York, Toronto, Melbourne and Bombay.
2. Attanagalu-Vansa or The History of The Temple of Attanagalla. tr. by James D'Alwis, M.R.A.S. Colombo.
3. Book of The Discipline (Vinaya-Pitaka,) Vol.I. tr. by I. B. Horner, M.A. London. Humphrey Milford, Oxford University Press.
4. Dhammapada, tr. from Chinese by Samuel Beal. London. Trubner & Co., Ludgate Hill.
5. Dhammapada Commentary, Vols. I & III, tr. by Eugene Watsone Burlingame. Cambridge.
6. Dialogues of The Buddha, Vol. I. tr. by T. W. Rhys Davids. London. Oxford University Press.
7. Divyāvadāna, Edited by E. B. Cowell, M.A., And R. A. Neil, M.A. At The University Press. Cambridge.
8. Expositor, The (Atthasalini) ,Vol. I, tr. by Maung Tin, M.A., London. Published For The Pali Text Society by The Oxford University Press.
9. Further Dialogue of The Buddha, Vol. II, tr. by Lord Chalmers, G.C.B. London. Humphrey Milford, Oxford University Press, Amen Corner, E.C.
10. Gandavyuha Sūtra, Edited by Daisetz Teitaro Suzaki And Hoki Idzumi, parts. I & II.
11. Geschichte des Buddhismus in Indien. by Tāranātha. tr. by Schiefner. St. Petersburg.
12. Jātaka Stories or The Buddha's Former Birth, The, Vol. I, by Robert Chalmers, M.A., & Vol. II, by W. H. D. Rouse, M.A., & Vol. III. by H. T. Francis, M.A., & R. A. Neil, M.A. Cambridge, At the University Press.
13. Lalita Vistara, tr. by Dr. Rajendra Lal Mitra, LL.D., C.I.E. At Baptist Mission Press, Calcutta.
14. Majjhimanikāya, Vol. II. tr. by Brikkhu Silacara.
15. Manual of Buddhism in its Modern Development. tr. from Singhalese Mss. by R. Spence Hardy, London.
16. Psalms Of The Early Buddhists (Psalms of The Sisters). By Mrs. Rhys Davids, M.A., London. Published For The Pali Text Society. By Henry Frowde, Oxford University Press, Warehouse, Amen Corner. E.C.

17. Romantic Legend of Śākya Buddha, tr. by Samuel Beal, London, Trubner & Co.
18. Saddharma-Puṇḍarika, tr. by H. Kern, At the Clarendon Press. Oxford.
19. She. R. A. B. Dong-Bu or Prajñā Dāna, by Lu-Trub (Nagarjuna. tr. by Major W. I. Campbell, C.I.E., Calcutta. Printed At the Baptist Mission Press And Published by the Calcutta University.
20. Vinaya Texts, Part I. to III. tr. by T. W. Rhys Davids and Hermann Oldenberg, At the Clarendon Press. Oxford.

F. Foreign Sources :—

(a) Chinese Source :—
1. A Record of Buddhistic Kingdoms (399–414, A.D.), by Fa-Hian. tr. by James Legge, M.A., LL.D. At the Clarendon Press, Oxford.
2. A Record of Buddhistic Practices, by I-Tsing, tr. by Takakusu.

(b) Greek Source :—
1. Indian Travels of Apollonius of Tyana And The Indian Embassies to Rome, by Osmond De Beauvoir Priaulx, London

(c) Arabian Sources :—

1. Ancient Account of India and China by Two Mahommedan Travellers, tr. by Eusebiur Reunando.

G. Archaelogical Sources :—

1. Cave Temples of India, by Dr. James Fergusson, & James Burges, London. W. H, Allen & Co.
2. Corpus Inscriptionum Indicarum, Vol. I. Inscriptions of Asoka. by E. Hultzsch, Ph.D.,
3. History of Fine Art in India And Ceylon. by Vincent Smith, At Clarendon Press. Oxford.

H. Other Secondary Sources :—

1. Ancient Geography of India, by Sir Alexander Cunningham, edited by Surendra Nath Majumdar Sastri, M.A., P.R.S. Calcutta, Chakravorty & Chatterjee & Co.
2. Educational Ideals in Kālidāsa's India, by Dr. Debendra Chandra Das Gupta, M.A., (Calif), Ed.D. (Calif) Prabuddha Bharat, 1942.
3. Essay on The Gunadhya And The Bṛhatkathā, by Felix Lacote, tr. Rajasabha Bhushana, Rev. A. M. Tabru, At the Bangalore Press,
4. Essays, by Michael De Montaigne, tr. by C. Cotton,

5. History of Indian Literature, Vol. II, by Maurice Winternitz, Ph.D. tr. by Mrs. S. Ketkar And Miss. H. Kohn, B.A. At the University Press, Calcutta.
6. Life of Hemacandra, The, By Dr. Bühler. Vidyābhavana, Visva-Bharati, Santiniketan. Published by The Adhisthata Singhi Jaina Jñānapitha.
7. Manu And His Educational Philosophy, by Dr. Debendra Chandra Das Gupta, Prabuddha Bharata. Feb. & March, 1943.
8. Principles of Human Geography, by E. Huntington and S. W. Cushing. 4th edition, John Wiley.
9. Rāsa Mālā or Hindu Annals Of The Province of Guzerat in Western India. Vol. I. & II, By Alexander Kinloch Forbes. London. Richardson Brothers.